AMERICAN TRANSCENDENTALISM,
1830–1860
An Intellectual Inquiry

American Transcendentalism, 1830–1860

An Intellectual Inquiry

by
Paul F. Boller, Jr.

G. P. PUTNAM'S SONS, NEW YORK
CAPRICORN BOOKS, NEW YORK

for Dick and Ksenija

Contents

Preface

WHAT follows is a survey of American Transcendentalism, from the 1830's to the Civil War. The major
emphasis is on the nineteenth-century cluster of ideas
known as the New Views; and the point of view is that of a
twentieth-century writer who regards himself as partly
Emersonian and partly Deweyan, partly Transcendentalist and partly empiricist. I take for granted the colossal
importance of the scientific method in enabling us to
generalize meaningfully about the empirical world and
turn it to fruitful human purposes. But I also believe that
there are irreducible (even unanalyzable) elements in
human experience which transcend verbal and conceptual formulations and elude the statistical and mathematical formulations of natural science, but which are the
major sources of creativity. As to methodology, I have
tried to follow William James's procedure in separating
existential analysis from critical evaluation and letting
the Transcendentalists speak as much as possible for
themselves before confronting them with the "superior
wisdom" of the 1970's. The first five chapters of this
book therefore are mostly devoted to recounting the
story of the movement and examining its ideas, and the
last chapter to deciding what is transient and what permanent in the Transcendental vision (though recogniz-

ing that standards of transience and permanence themselves shift with the passage of time). The purposes of the book, then, are both historical and transcendental. I have wanted to discuss critically but sympathetically the Transcendental movement in all its ramifications (religious radicalism, philosophical antecedents and affinities, major concepts, reform activities, and optimistic outlook), and also to analyze Transcendental ideas for their intrinsic interest and significance for all times and places. The book combines synthesis with explication and evaluation and it is primarily an intellectual rather than an economic, aesthetic, or literary inquiry.

The American Transcendentalists were enormously well-read and extraordinarily articulate. They wrote letters, journals, lectures, essays, poems, sketches, and memoirs in abundance and there is a massive treasure of fascinating material available for exploration, analysis, interpretation, and criticism. The historiography of Transcendentalism has been equally prodigious. There are few nooks and crannies left in the movement which have not been explored with infinite care and in loving detail by at least one investigator. The Transcendentalists have been perhaps the most exegeticized (they would have been appalled by it) group of literary intellectuals in American history. There has been at least as much written about Emerson as by him (though we are now down to examining his wastebasket, with, it must be acknowledged, illuminating results); in Thoreau's case, probably twice as much. My emphasis has been on Emerson and Thoreau for obvious reasons, though I have tried to do as much as space permitted with their extremely gifted associates: Margaret Fuller, Bronson Alcott, Theodore Parker, George Ripley, Orestes Brownson, Frederic Hedge, William H. Channing, James F. Clarke, Elizabeth Peabody, Christopher Cranch, John S. Dwight, and Ellery Channing. It would be hard to generalize about Emerson and Thoreau; but it is simply impossible to generalize with facility about Emerson, Thoreau, and all their friends and colleagues together, though I think the attempt is worth making. I have spent most of my account on the heyday of the Transcendental movement and on its intellectual life. Whether Transcendental ideas, the primary interest of this study, are still relevant to contemporary concerns readers will determine for themselves. I have proceeded on the assumption that they are.

I would like to thank John P. Diggins, Professor of History at the University of California, Irvine, for his critical reading of the first draft of this book and for his thoughtful suggestions for putting it into final form. I would also like to thank the countless young people with whom it has been my privilege for many years to discuss Transcendentalism in the classroom at Southern Methodist University, the University of Texas, and the University of Massachusetts in Boston, and from whom I learned fresh ways of viewing the Transcendentalists as well as the world of which I am a part.

PAUL F. BOLLER, JR.
Boston, Massachusetts
January, 1974

Introduction

IN the fall of 1836, the Transcendental Club held its first meeting at George Ripley's home in Boston, met irregularly for the next three or four years at various places, and then dropped out of existence. Some people thought it was typically transcendental: without constitution, dues, chairman, officers, regular members, or settled time and place of meeting, and given to airy speculations. It didn't even have a name at first. Some members called it the "Symposium" in honor of Plato; others referred to it as "Hedge's Club" because it tended to meet whenever Frederic Henry Hedge, Bangor minister, came down from Maine to visit Boston. But outsiders, amused by (and somewhat disdainful of) the elevated discussions that took place whenever the group assembled, started calling it the Transcendental Club and the name stuck. When the story got out that someone had asked Bronson Alcott at one meeting whether "omnipotence abnegates attributes," critics were convinced that the name was entirely appropriate.

Alcott, with Ralph Waldo Emerson one of the club's most faithful members, described it as "a company of earnest persons enjoying conversations on high themes and having much in common." At the second meeting, in Alcott's house, the discussion centered on a topic proposed by Emerson: " 't was pity that in this Titanic continent, where nature is so grand, genius should be so tame." The Transcendentalists were always to be concerned about the derivativeness of so much of American culture. Later sessions dwelt on law, truth, individuality, theology, Providence, mysticism, pantheism, and personality, also perennial topics of interest to the Transcendentalists. The original members of the club were mostly Unitarian ministers or ex-ministers, but they soon welcomed college professors, farmers, mechanics, and merchants to their meetings. And, in an unusual action for the day, they also invited women to attend: Margaret Fuller, Elizabeth Peabody, and Sophia Ripley. It was a relatively young group: people mainly in their twenties and thirties. The somewhat thorny Henry David Thoreau at twenty-two was the youngest to attend and the venerable Unitarian divine William Ellery Channing, who came once, was the oldest at fifty-seven. At the meetings, Frederic Hedge, according to one observer, supplied the trained philosophic mind; James Freeman Clarke, the philanthropic comprehensiveness; Theodore Parker, the robust energy; Orestes Brownson, the combative vigor; William H. Channing, young nephew of William Ellery, the lofty enthusiasm; George Ripley, the practical understanding; Alcott, the pure idealism; and Emerson, the penetrating insight.

To some people the Transcendentalists seemed a forbidding group. Emerson, perhaps the wisest of them all, was generous and kindly enough (and frequently called "angelic"), but extremely reserved and dignified and, as he rather regretfully admitted, not given to easy camaraderie. Thoreau, his young friend, was skeptical, blunt, and acerbic; a kind of Yankee Diogenes who (said Oliver Wendell Holmes) insisted on nibbling his asparagus at the wrong end. Margaret Fuller was brilliant, headstrong, and outspoken; she once announced that she found no intellect in America comparable to her own. When Elizabeth Peabody, who ran a bookshop in Boston which was a gathering place for literati and reformers, told her that she walked into church as if she felt superior to everybody there, she exclaimed unhesitatingly: "Well, I did feel so." Theodore Parker impressed everyone with his vast energy and his even vaster erudition; he had a canine appetite, it was clear, for devouring new information in a dozen languages. Orestes Brownson was the polemicist of the group; willing and eager to take on all comers, he was convinced of the unassailability of each new position which he adopted from time to time. Even the Transcendentalists found him formidable and some of them were pleased when he stopped coming to meetings of the club.

Hostile observers complained that the Transcendentalists were arrogant. Young George Curtis saw some of them sitting around in Emerson's library in Concord one day, dignified and erect, as if to ask (so he imagined): "Who will now proceed to say the finest thing that has ever been said?" But he soon learned that his initial impression was mistaken and he came later to write about them with sympathy and affection. The Transcendentalists were unquestionably proud; they admired strength, courage, self-confidence, and independence of mind. But they were also modest, for they were relentlessly self-critical, endlessly eager to expand their knowledge, experience, and understanding of life, and painfully aware of the deficiencies in depth, scope, and originality of the American culture which was their heritage. They were also on the whole a generous and compassionate group; they wanted to help others to find themselves and put their talents to use in enriching American life. They were especially interested in young men and women of promise and they were anxious to encourage intellectual and spiritual growth in the emerging generation. In a lecture on "Human Life" given in Boston in December, 1838, Emerson explained Transcendental aspirations for American youth:

> This *deliquium*, this ossification of the soul, is the Fall of Man. The redemption is lodged in the heart of youth. To every young man and woman the world puts the same question, Wilt thou become one of us? And to this question the soul in each of them says heartily, No. . . . No matter though the young heart do not yet understand itself, do not know well what it wants, and so contents itself with saying, No, No, to unamiable tediousness, or breaks out into sallies of extravagance. There is hope in extravagance; there is none in routine.
>
> The hostile attitude of young persons toward society makes them very undesirable companions to their friends, querulous, opinionative, impracticable; and it makes them unhappy in their solitude. If it continues too long it makes shiftless and morose men. Yet, on the whole, this crisis which comes in so forbidding and painful shape in the life of each earnest man has nothing in it that need alarm or confound us. In some form the question comes to each: Will you fulfill the demands of the soul, or will you yield to the conventions of the world? None can escape the challenge.

Then, addressing young people directly, Emerson exclaimed:

> But why need you sit there, pale, and pouting, or why with such a mock-tragic air affect discontent and superiority? The bugbear of society is such only until you have accepted your own law. Then all

omens are good, all stars auspicious, all men your allies, all parts of life take order and beauty.

Emerson realized that older people tended to distrust him and that young people admired him. The young were clearly his main audience; they came to his house in Concord to have earnest discussions with him and they sent him letters from all over the United States and from Europe and Asia as well. Even some of the Transcendentalists thought they worshipped him too blindly and Parker grumbled about youthful "Emersonidae" with bad manners. But Emerson never demeaned the young by seeking their adoration; nor did he insult them by flattery. He took them seriously by criticizing as well as encouraging them. He wanted to open their eyes to the beauties, dignities, and opportunities of life, present them with lofty goals, and stimulate them to noble behavior and high achievement.

Emerson's associates agreed in the main with his hopes for the young, but there was nothing monolithic about Transcendentalism. James F. Clarke once quipped that the Transcendental Club was called "the club of the like-minded; I suppose because no two of us thought alike." The Transcendentalists were not a compact group; there was no party line and they did not see eye to eye on everything. Emerson liked Thoreau's free and erect mind but was vexed by his penchant for paradox; he hailed Alcott as an original thinker, but sometimes thought he was a "tedious Archangel." Margaret Fuller worshipped Emerson, but complained (as did other Transcendentalists) that he "always seemed to be on stilts," and Emerson for his part found her a little too impetuous for his nature. George Ripley was disappointed in Emerson for refusing to join the Brook Farm Community and he deplored Alcott's humorlessness.

Thoreau was repelled by Ripley's experiment at Brook Farm, but Emerson took a friendly interest in it. Brownson sent his son there but his enthusiasm for Ripley's enterprise was highly restrained. The unworldly though perspicacious Alcott observed the Concord group with affection and considerable shrewdness and went his own merry way (with occasional financial assistance from Emerson) serenely and imperturbably (most of the time). Ripley found strengths and limitations in his Transcendental friends and they in him. Thoreau was mainly impressed by the limitations. Theodore Parker (whom Emerson called "our Savonarola") told John Sullivan Dwight, the musician of the group: "You love vagueness, mistaking the indefinite for the Infinite." Dwight told Parker: "You write, you read, you talk, you think, in a hurry, for fear of not getting all." And so it went. Still, amid all the rumbling and grumbling, the Transcendentalists were in essential accord on fundamentals; they were familiar with each other's work, commented on it freely, and exchanged opinions amicably enough most of the time. There was both conflict and consensus among the Transcendentalists. There were also unresolved tensions in their thinking: parochial prejudices but cosmopolitan concerns; ambivalence toward social action; a passion for amassing empirical data to bolster intuitive certainties; and an unceasing alternation (especially in Emerson's case) between monism and pluralism, universalism and individualism, mysticism and empiricism, religion and science, society and solitude, reform and repose. James Russell Lowell was perceptive in seeing Emerson as a kind of "Plotinus-Montaigne." There was something of mystic and skeptic in most of the Transcendentalists.

The heyday of Transcendentalism was in the 1830's and 1840's and to later generations of Americans its interior life has seemed of greatest interest. The external story was not spectacular. It concerned mainly young people in the Boston and Cambridge area during the Age of Jackson who were mostly educated at Harvard, theologically trained, middle-class, and Puritan and Unitarian in background. A brief chronology would perhaps begin in 1832, when Emerson left the ministry, and proceed swiftly to 1836, the *annus mirabilis* of the movement, during which Emerson published *Nature*, the Transcendentalists' Bible, Ripley published *Discourses on the Philosophy of Religion*, Brownson published *New Views of Christianity, Society, and the Church*, Alcott published *Record of Conversations on the Gospel* (based on classroom discussions in his Temple School in Boston and provoking severe criticism), and the Transcendental Club met for the first time; then move to 1837, when Emerson delivered his Phi Beta Kappa address on "The American Scholar" at Harvard, which Lowell called "an event without any former parallel in our literary annals"; to 1838, the year of Emerson's Divinity School Address at Harvard which touched off a great storm in religious circles; 1840 (the founding of the *Dial*, a Transcendental magazine which "enjoyed its obscurity," to use Emerson's words, for four years); 1841 (the launching of Ripley's Brook Farm experiment); 1842 (Alcott's experiment at Fruitlands); 1845 (Thoreau went to Walden); and 1846 (Thoreau went to jail). The Transcendental story, externally, centered largely on conversations, exchanges of letters, lecture engagements, publication dates, and journal entries. After the passage of the Fugitive Slave Act in 1850, however, the Transcendentalists found themselves, somewhat to their own surprise, becoming increasingly involved in abolitionism, attending rallies, participating in demonstrations, and delivering speeches at antislavery meetings.

Transcendentalism was a religious, philosophical, and literary movement and it is located in the history of

American thought as post-Unitarian and freethinking in religion, as Kantian and idealistic in philosophy, and as Romantic and individualistic in literature. The religious impulse, however, was primary; piety concerned the Transcendentalists, especially in the beginning, even more than moralism. By the 1830's, the Unitarian concensus which educated and established people in the Boston area found comfortable and satisfying had lost its emotional appeal for thoughtful and sensitive young people. It "seemed to relate too much to outward things, not enough to the inward pious life," Parker recalled. "It is negative, cold, lifeless," complained Brownson, "and all advanced minds among Unitarians are dissatisfied with it, and are craving something higher, better, more living, and lifegiving." Emerson thought that Unitarian affirmations had become largely verbal. "We die of words," he exclaimed. "We are hanged, drawn and quartered by dictionaries. . . . When shall we attain to be real, and be born into the new heaven and earth of nature and truth?" The Transcendental revolt began as a quest for new ways of conceiving the human condition to replace old ways that no longer carried conviction. It also involved the search for new vocations since the clerical profession for which so many of the Transcendentalists had been trained had ceased to be a live option for most of them. Transcendentalism, in short, was mainly an enterprise undertaken by bright young Unitarians to find meaning, pattern, and purpose in a universe no longer managed by a genteel and amiable Unitarian God.

There was, to be sure, no one precise "cause" for the genesis of Transcendentalism. With the New Views, as with other patterns of ideas that suddenly catch on with sizable numbers of people, chance, coincidence, and the accidental concatenation of several independent events probably explains what happened. (Whether there is a meaningful pattern in coincidences, as Emerson in his day and Arthur Koestler in our own have contended, remains an open question for this particular student of ideas.) Several tendencies of thought and action seem to have converged in the 1830's in New England to precipitate the solution which we call Transcendentalism: the steady erosion of Calvinism; the progressive secularization of modern thought under the impact of science and technology; the emergence of a Unitarian intelligentsia with the means, leisure, and training to pursue literature and scholarship; the increasing insipidity and irrelevance of liberal religion to questing young minds; the intrusion of the machine into the New England garden and the disruption of the old order by the burgeoning industrialism; the impact of European ideas on Americans traveling and studying abroad; the appearance of talented and energetic young people like Emerson and Thoreau on the scene; and the imperatives of logic itself for those who take ideas seriously (the impossibility, for instance, of accepting modern science without revising traditional religious views). Perhaps youth—if it is serious enough, sufficiently talented, adequately informed, and willing to work hard—is the indispensable element for stirring the various tendencies of thought into a new heady brew for the emerging generation to quaff. The Transcendentalists, at any rate, seem to have thought so. They were not radicals in the political sense; but the questions they asked of their country and their age were devastating. "We come down with free thinking into the dear institutions," Emerson mused, "and at once make carnage among them." Many of the questions the Transcendentalists posed—and the answers they proposed—have passed into the mainstream of American critical thought and continue to challenge America's more conventional wisdom.

For its participants, Transcendentalism was an exhilarating experience. Though they all knew heartbreak, pain, frustration, and failure, they were an astonishingly happy and appreciative group, at least if judged by present-day standards. Parker criticized the Unitarian establishment of his day because it preached "duty, duty! work, work!" without also proclaiming "joy, joy! delight, delight!" Today, curiously, if one wishes to recapture the feeling of excitement, challenge, adventure, and sheer wonder that the Transcendentalists found in the universe, he must turn to contemporary physics and astronomy (rather than to the humanities), both of which are seething with new discoveries and fresh insights. Or he must turn to the field of space exploration. In the 1970's, American astronauts, viewing planet earth from lunar perspectives, experienced the deep underlying sense of awe and wonder that the Transcendentalists had regarded as essential to the full life. "I completely lost my identity as an American astronaut," reported one astronaut of his experience in outer space. "I felt a part of everyone and everything sweeping past me below." "You don't look down at the world as an American," said another astronaut, "but as a human being."

But the Transcendentalists didn't need to go to the moon to experience the wonder of things. They saw it everywhere about them. Transcendentalism meant rising a little above conventional use and wont; it meant breaking out of habitual ways of conceiving things to some degree and trying to view reality with what has been called an innocent eye. "These roses under my window make no reference to former roses or to better ones," averred Emerson; "they are for what they are; they exist with God today. There is no time to them. There is simply the rose." (Gertrude Stein put it more succinctly: "A rose is a rose is a rose.") The notion of an "innocent eye" is no doubt a fiction; it is simply impossible for us to perceive anything in complete isolation from our past experiences and we inevitably impose some kind of mental framework on all our data of perception. But the Transcendentalists were aware of this; they knew their Kant. What they did think was possible, however, was to go a little beyond the received wisdom of the day and to take a fresh look at the world about us. If people did so, they insisted, they might to their surprise see beauty, dignity, grandeur, and miracle where before had been only convention and routine. "The young mortal," wrote Emerson in "Illusions,"

> enters the hall of the firmament; there is he alone with them [the gods] alone, they pouring on him benedictions and gifts, and beckoning him up to their thrones. On the instant, and incessantly, fall snow-storms of illusions. He fancies himself in a vast crowd which sways this way and that and whose movement and doings he must obey: he fancies himself poor, orphaned, insignificant. The mad crowd drives hither and thither, now furiously commanding this thing to be done, now that. What is he that he should resist their will, and think or act for himself? Every moment new changes and new showers of deceptions to baffle and distract him. And when, by and by, for an instant, the air clears and the cloud lifts a little, there are the gods still sitting around him on their thrones,—they alone with him alone.

AMERICAN TRANSCENDENTALISM,
1830–1860
An Intellectual Inquiry

CHAPTER ONE

Religious Radicalism

AMERICAN Transcendentalism began as a revolt against historical Christianity. It developed as a protest movement within the Unitarian Church in New England (particularly in the Boston area) during the 1830's and its most prominent spokesmen were Unitarian clergymen, like Ralph Waldo Emerson, who had studied at the Harvard Divinity School. In its deepest reaches Transcendentalism was a quest for authentic religious experience. It rejected forms, creeds, rites, and verbal explanations and sought to penetrate to the heart of things by a direct, immediate encounter with reality. Its objective, Emerson announced, was an original relation with the universe.

"Whenever the pulpit is usurped by a formalist," complained Emerson in his famous Divinity School Address, "then is the worshipper defrauded and disconsolate." Then he went on to express his Transcendental discontents with the churches of his day:

I once heard a preacher who sorely tempted me to say I would go to church no more. . . . A snow-storm was falling around us. The snow-storm was real, the

1

preacher merely spectral, and the eye felt the sad contrast in looking at him, and then out of the window behind him into the beautiful meteor of the snow. He had lived in vain. He had no one word intimating that he had laughed or wept, was married or in love, had been commended, or cheated, or chagrined. If he had ever lived and acted, we were none the wiser for it. . . . This man had ploughed and planted and talked and bought and sold; he had read books; he had eaten and drunken; his head aches, his heart throbs; he smiles and suffers; yet was there not a surmise, a hint, in all the discourse, that he had ever lived at all. Not a line did he draw out of real history.

Emerson was thinking of Barzillai Frost, minister of the Unitarian church in Concord, when he composed these words; but he regarded Frost's bland sermonizing as typical of "the thin porridge or cold tea of Unitarianism." Six years earlier, when he was only twenty-nine, he had resigned his pastorate at the Second Church in Boston because the pastoral duties irked him and because he could no longer conscientiously administer the sacrament of the Lord's Supper, even in its most attenuated form; and he had gone on to find his true vocation as Transcendentalist lecturer, essayist, poet, philosopher, and editor.

Emerson was not the only Unitarian minister to leave the church at this time. George Ripley resigned from the Purchase Street Church in Boston with similar discontents in 1840 and went on to found the Brook Farm Association. Christopher P. Cranch preached for a time after leaving Harvard and then abandoned the ministry for poetry and landscape painting. John S. Dwight also served as a minister only briefly and then left the profession to become a musical journalist. Like Emerson, all of these men had attended the Divinity School at Cambridge, the Unitarians' pride and joy, and all of them had come, mainly under Emerson's influence, to adopt what were called the "New Views" about religion. There were, to be sure, ministers who sympathized with the New Views but who continued their pastorates. Frederic Henry Hedge of Bangor, Maine, and James Freeman Clarke of Louisville, Kentucky, were among the best known. Theodore Parker, one of the most outspoken exponents of the New Views, also remained in the church, though orthodox Unitarians would have minded it not a bit had he defected. In addition to clergymen with Transcendental leanings, there were countless laymen—young men and women brought up as Unitarians—who were dissatisfied with the church and receptive to the New Views. "I have let myself be cheated out of my Sunday," lamented Margaret Fuller after attending a Unitarian service and hearing a boring sermon on the deficiencies of Calvinism. "That crowd of upturned faces, with their look of unintelligent complacency!" Her feelings were widely shared by young Unitarians in Boston and Cambridge. "Pale negations," "corpse-cold," "lifeless," "formalistic"—these became common complaints about Unitarianism among the young in eastern Massachusetts in the 1830's. Even William Ellery Channing, the "grey eminence" of Boston Unitarianism, acknowledged that a "heart-withering philosophy" pervaded his church, though he had substantial reservations about the New Views.

Emerson's Divinity School Address

In 1838, Emerson stirred up a storm when he carried the New Views into the very citadel of New England Unitarianism, the Divinity School at Cambridge. Asked by members of the senior class to address them at graduation time, Emerson decided to take the opportunity to express opinions about religion which he had been turning over in his mind ever since leaving the ministry in 1832. His address, which touched off an acrimonious controversy when it was published, was mild enough in tone and moderately phrased. (Emerson, Oliver Wendell Holmes observed, was "an iconoclast without a hammer, who took down our idols from their pedestals so tenderly that it seemed like an act of worship.") The occasion, moreover, could scarcely have been less spectacular: six graduating seniors, a handful of teachers, and a few friends gathered in the small chapel on the second floor of Divinity Hall on Sunday evening, July 15. But what Emerson said that night seemed shocking to respectable Unitarians in New England and to orthodox Christians everywhere. Though he later minimized the controversy he had started as a "storm in our washbowl," it was much more than that. His Divinity School Address became one of the basic documents of the Transcendental movement and it was to have a profound effect on American religious thought in the nineteenth century.

Emerson began his address by celebrating what he liked to call the "moral sentiment," that is, intuitive insight into moral and spiritual laws, which could never be received at second hand. Every person, Emerson told the students, possesses this sentiment of virtue; it represents the "indwelling Supreme Spirit" in all men and women and it is "the essence of all religion. . . ." The Christian church, according to Emerson, had come to neglect the moral sentiment and in so doing had fallen into two grievous errors: it exaggerated the personal and miraculous authority of Jesus Christ and it looked upon revelation itself as past and dead and confined to Biblical times. The "assumption that the age of inspiration is past, that the Bible is closed; the fear of degrading the character of Jesus by representing him as a man;

—indicate with sufficient clearness the falsehood of our theology." But Jesus himself knew better:

> He spoke of miracles; for he felt that man's life was a miracle, and all that man doth, and he knew that this daily miracle shines as the character ascends. But the word Miracle, as pronounced by Christian churches, gives a false impression; it is Monster. It is not one with the blowing clover and the falling rain.

Erroneous views of miracles and of revelation, said Emerson, were responsible for a decaying church and waning belief. And the only remedy for the erosion of faith was to recognize the reality of the moral sentiment and our ability, through it, to achieve "eternal revelation in the heart" today, as Jesus did ages ago. Avoid secondary knowledge, Emerson advised the would-be ministers; dare to love God without mediator or veil, and in preaching try to acquaint people at first hand with Deity. It was the office of a true teacher, he declared, to "show us that God is, not was; that He speaketh, not spake." True Christianity, Emerson asserted, rested on "a faith like Christ's in the infinitude of man."

Young Theodore Parker, ordained only a few days before, was enthralled by Emerson's address: a "Sermon on the Mount," he called it. "So beautiful, so just, so true, and terribly sublime," he wrote in his journal afterwards. The Reverend Henry Ware, Jr., Emerson's former associate at the Second Church in Boston and now professor of divinity at Harvard, was considerably less impressed, though he had some words of praise for Emerson that evening. Overnight, however, he had second thoughts. He was especially bothered by what appeared to be Emerson's identification of God with the physical and moral laws governing creation and by his apparent tendency toward pantheism. The next day he wrote to

Emerson, warning that some of the things he had said the night before worked against the authority and influence of Christianity. He appreciated Emerson's "lofty ideas and beautiful images of spiritual life," he hastened to add, but he was concerned about the general drift of Emerson's thought and he urged him to retract or modify some of his statements. But Emerson wrote back calmly: "I thought I would not pay the nobleness of my friends so mean a compliment as to suppress my opposition to their supposed views out of fear of offense."

That fall, still upset by his former colleague's views, Ware preached a sermon at Harvard on "The Personality of God," in which he averred that denial of personality to God "amounts to a virtual denial of God." God, he said, was more than the principles and attributes, physical and moral, making up the universe; he was Creator, King, Lawgiver, and Father. "There is a personal God," insisted Ware, "or there is none." He also expressed horror at Emerson's suggestion that the words of Plato or Mahomet or Luther were just as inspired as those of Jesus; such a view, he declared, not only destroyed Jesus' authority; it also made all truth a revelation and all men revealers and thus in effect destroyed the uniqueness of the Christian revelation. Ware sent Emerson a printed copy of his sermon, but again Emerson refused to be drawn into controversy. Describing himself as a "chartered libertine" who was "free to worship and free to rail," Emerson told *le bon Henri* (as he called him) that he "did not feel any disposition to depart from my habitual tendency, that you shall say your thought, whilst I say mine." He also explained that:

> . . . there is no scholar less willing or less able than myself to be a polemic. I could not give an account of myself, if challenged. I could not possibly give you one of the "arguments" you cruelly hint at, on which

any doctrine of mine stands, for I do not know what arguments mean in reference to any expression of a thought. I delight in telling what I think; but if you ask me how I dare say so, or why it is so, I am the most helpless of mortal men.

Emerson abhorred disputatious confrontation. Engaging in polemics, he thought, was a poor way to advance the truth. It was one of the blunders of egotism: it stressed scoring points and intruding one's person too much onto the scene. Emerson had had his honest say and he could see no point in expending efforts to make sure that he was personally understood. His wife (whom he liked to call "Asia") agreed with his determination to remain silent amid criticism. "What said my brave Asia concerning the paragraph writers, today?" wrote Emerson playfully in his journal:

. . . that "this whole practice of self-justification and recrimination betwixt literary men seemed every whit as low as the quarrels of the Paddies." Then said I, "But what will you say, excellent Asia, when my smart article comes out in the paper, in reply to Mr. A. and Dr. B.?" "Why, then," answered she, "I shall feel the first emotion of féar and sorrow on your account."—"But do you know," I asked, "how many fine things I have thought of to say to these fighters. They are too good to be lost." "Then," rejoined the queen, "there is some merit in being silent."

But if Emerson refused to argue his point of view, neither would he soften the expression of his opinions in the interest of peace. When he was preparing the Divinity School Address for publication, Elizabeth Peabody, Boston teacher and bookseller, who had heard and liked it, asked him whether he intended to print the phrase

"friend of man," referring to Jesus, with a capital "F."
"No," said Emerson, "directly I put that large F in they
will all go to sleep." When she suggested that he reinsert
in the printed copy a passage warning against irrever-
ence toward Jesus which he had omitted during the
delivery because of the pressure of time, Emerson reflected for a moment and then said: "No; these gentlemen have committed themselves against what I did read,
and it would not be courteous or fair to spring upon
them this passage now, which would convict them of an
unwarranted inference."

When Emerson's address reached print, there was an
immediate blast against it in the Boston *Daily Advertiser*
for August 27 signed by A.N. A.N., as everyone knew,
was Andrews Norton, New England Unitarianism's leading theologian, former professor of sacred literature in
the Divinity School, and now in retirement at Shady Hill.
Author of the three-volume *Evidences of the Genuineness of
the Gospels*, the first volume of which appeared in 1837
and which found the basic evidence for the Christian
religion in Jesus' miracles, Norton recognized that
Emerson had called in question the foundations of Unitarian theology when he substituted the moral sentiment
for miracles as the basis for religion and he knew he
could not remain silent. He was exasperated, moreover,
to see Emerson doing what Norton's old foes among
Calvinistic Congregationalists had been predicting for
Unitarians all along: moving from the liberal position of
New England Unitarianism to a position practically outside the Christian camp itself. In his piece for the
Advertiser, Norton pronounced a "general anathema" on
such freethinkers as Harriet Martineau, Percy Bysshe
Shelley, Victor Cousin, Thomas Carlyle, and Friedrich
Schleiermacher, and he then denounced Emerson as the
latest enemy of principles which he regarded as the
foundation of human society and happiness. Emerson,

according to Norton, not only rejected Christian revelation in his "incoherent rhapsody"; he also left serious doubts about whether he even believed in God. Norton had no doubt that "silly women" and "silly young men" might be attracted to Emerson's views, but he wanted one point to be clear: no one could share Emerson's ideas and take on the role of Christian teacher without committing a falsehood. Norton absolved Harvard authorities from all blame for "this insult to religion," but he did regard those students who invited Emerson to speak as "accessories," though perhaps innocent ones, to the commission of a grave offense.

Emerson was struck by the "feminine vehemence" of Norton's assault; but the response of Cornelius Felton, professor of Greek at Harvard, was even more vehement. Felton found Emerson's discourse "full of extravagance and over-weening self-confidence, ancient errors disguised in misty rhetoric, and theories which would overturn society and resolve the world into chaos." John G. Palfrey, dean of the Divinity School, fully shared Felton's indignation and he called Emerson's address part folly and part downright atheism. The reaction of the *Christian Examiner*, the official organ of New England Unitarianism, was less frenetic but just as disapproving. So far as Emerson's views were intelligible, said the *Examiner*, they were "utterly distasteful to the instructors of the School, and to Unitarian ministers generally, by whom they are esteemed to be neither good divinity nor good sense." The editors went on to propose a faculty veto over Harvard Divinity students' choice of speakers in the future. ("The shepherds of Harvard," said Ezra Stiles Gannett, Channing's conservative assistant at the Federal Street Church in Boston, "could hardly be expected to allow the wolf to carry off the lambs in their very presence, even at the invitation of the innocents themselves.")

If the editors of the *Examiner* and other Unitarians found Emerson's ideas misty and obscure as well as up-setting, orthodox Calvinists never had any doubts about what Emerson was up to. "We have read it," wrote two Presbyterian theologians of "Mr. Emerson's rhapsody" (in the *Biblical Repertory and Princeton Review*), and "we want words with which to express our sense of the non-sense and impiety which pervade it." Lamenting that the pantheistic philosophy had set its "cloven foot" in America, Charles Hodge, professor at the Princeton Theological Seminary, exclaimed in the pages of the same journal: "If it was not for its profaneness, what could be more ludicrous than Mr. Emerson's Address?" As the storm raged, Emerson kept his peace: "Let me never fall into the vulgar mistake of dreaming that I am persecuted whenever I am contradicted," he confided to his *Journal*. In the agitation that his address stirred up, Emerson himself, noted Holmes, "had little more than the part of Patroclus when the Greeks and Trojans fought over his body."

Though Emerson remained silent, Norton was unwilling to let the matter drop. He found it hard to forgive Emerson for putting the Unitarians on the spot with non-Unitarian Christians. By uttering heresies at Harvard, Emerson had exposed Unitarians like Norton to taunts by orthodox Congregationalists that Emersonian infidelity was simply the logical consequence of Unitarian liberalism, which they had always regarded as a halfway house to infidelity. It was all very clear to the orthodox: when Unitarians like Norton had discarded the doctrines of the Trinity, original sin, and predestined election by the grace of God, they had abandoned the heart of the Christian religion. In orthodox eyes, the faith of Liberal Christians (as the Unitarians were called) in human reason and in the potentiality of all people to achieve salvation through their own efforts was scarcely distinguishable from German and French rationalism. It hardly helped, they thought, to cling to Jesus' miracles when practically everything else uniquely Christian had been cast aside. But Norton, and Liberal Christians generally, thought the errors were all on the orthodox side. The Calvinists demanded too much in the way of belief, Unitarians argued; and by straining people's credulity, it was they, not the Unitarians, who opened the sluice gates to unbelief for intelligent and educated people. The Unitarians, after all, offered a decent, respectable, and enlightened religion for educated people: faith in a benevolent Deity, in the perfectibility of man, in good works, and in universal salvation resting on human efforts. And the evidence for these beliefs appeared —as those for Calvinist doctrines surely did not—in the New Testament. Was not Norton making a meticulous examination of this evidence in his massively researched volumes on the genuineness of the Christian gospel?

In 1839, Norton renewed his attack on Emerson in an address before the alumni of the Cambridge Divinity School on July 19. He reasserted the Unitarian position on Christian evidences and blistered Emerson's views as the "latest form of infidelity." In denying the historicity of Christian miracles, Norton declared, Emerson denied the truth of Christianity. Christianity, Norton insisted,

> was a revelation from God; and, in being so, it was itself a miracle. Christ was commissioned by God to speak to us in his name; and this is a miracle. No proof of this divine commission could be afforded, but through miraculous displays of God's power. Nothing is left that can be called Christianity if its miraculous character be denied.

Jesus, in other words, healed the lame and the blind, changed water into wine, walked on water, raised

Lazarus from the dead, and fed a multitude with a few loaves and fishes. His miraculous power to do these things was evidence that the truths he uttered were revelations from God, for "if there be a God, in the proper sense of the word, there can be no room for doubt, that he may act in a manner different from that in which he displays his power in the ordinary operations of nature." As a good Lockean, moreover, Norton regarded intuition as inadequate for establishing reliable knowledge; what was needed was empirical evidence for Christian truth. "We must use the same faculties, and adopt the same rules in judging concerning the facts of the world which we have not seen as concerning those of the world of which we have seen a very little." Jesus' miracles were objective evidence of the divine origin and authority of Christianity and no one, Norton thundered, could reject them without being guilty of "treachery towards God and man."

Ripley, Parker, and the Miracles Controversy

With the appearance of Norton's address in print, George Ripley, a Boston minister with considerable sympathy for the New Views, leaped into the fray. Ripley, who had had an unpleasant exchange with Norton about miracles in the Boston *Daily Advertiser* a couple of years earlier, was irked by the cavalier way in which Norton wrote off as unbelievers all who shared Emerson's views. To do this, he exclaimed, was to enforce the "exclusive principle," the very principle which Calvinists had applied to Unitarians earlier in the century when the latter cast overboard the Trinity and other orthodox Christian doctrines. Ripley recalled that Norton had once been a champion of mental freedom and had formerly reprimanded the orthodox for being so presumptuous as to define Christianity in such a way as

to exclude Unitarians. Your discourse, he told Norton,
was addressed

> to a body of Christians, whose prominent charac-
> teristic is the defense of freedom of mind,—of not
> only the right, but the duty, and of course, the power
> of private judgment, to the most unlimited extent.
> We have claimed to be the very Protestants of the
> Protestants; our watchword has been, "The people,
> and not the priest" . . . if the term "liberal Christian"
> is sacred and dear to any hearts among the
> breathing multitude around us, it is because we have
> discarded the lifeless formulas of the schools; be-
> cause we have sought to make Christianity a vital
> sentiment, instead of a barren tradition. . . .

As to miracles, Ripley confessed that he, personally, accepted them; but many sincere Christians, he reminded
Norton, found other evidences for Christianity far more
convincing: the character of Jesus, the excellence of his
teaching, the spirit of the Gospel, and the harmony of
Christian doctrines with man's higher nature. These
were all "internal evidences" and they were available to
the "intuitive perceptions" of all people. "There is something in the character of Christ," said Ripley, "which, to
an attentive reader of his history, is of more force than
ALL THE WEIGHT OF EXTERNAL evidence to prove
him DIVINE." Ripley thought that in modern English
theology only a few writers—those who were led by John
Locke's philosophy to attach undue value to external
evidence—still stressed miracles the way Norton did.
Ripley spent considerable space analyzing the Scriptures
to show that miracles weren't the only evidence of divine
revelation; but he also made a special point of the fact
that Norton's view turned the Christian religion into a
matter, largely, of exegesis: picking over Scriptural pas-

sages to determine which miracles were valid and which were not. (Even Norton didn't accept all of them as valid.) It was this very pedantry, Ripley sighed, that made Unitarianism seem so lifeless and mechanical to so many young people and drove them away from religion. But Christian truth, he said, had never been the monopoly of scholars, antiquaries, and exegetists; it had always been addressed to the intuitive perceptions of the average person. Norton was wrong in maintaining that the spiritual truths of Christianity were to be ascertained by the same method—accumulating external evidence—as the physical truths of natural science. The former rested on the heart and did not require extensive erudition for their apprehension. This was all that Spinoza, Schleiermacher, and Wilhelm Martin DeWette (whom Norton blamed in part for the newest infidelity) were saying about religion, Ripley insisted, and he took it upon himself to make a detailed defense of their views against Norton's aspersions on them toward the end of his pamphlet. In so doing, he got Norton—and the whole controversy over the New Views—off track.

Norton deigned to reply to Ripley only once. (Ripley directed three lengthy missives Norton's way before he was done.) In his response, he reiterated his belief that a revelation from God to man, authenticated by miracles, had been made by Jesus. He also dismissed as a metaphysical absurdity the supposition that it was possible to have direct perceptions of religious truths. But he devoted the bulk of his reply to bolstering up his original case against Spinoza, Schleiermacher, and DeWette; and Ripley, a student of German literature and theology who knew something about these men, felt obliged to respond in kind. His second letter produced massive quotations to show that Spinoza was no atheist and his third letter concentrated on upholding the Christian reputations of Schleiermacher and DeWette. At the same time he continued to insist that inward feeling or intuition was far superior to the senses in the apprehension of spiritual truth.

About this time Richard Hildreth, a Boston lawyer (and later a historian of the United States), decided to join Ripley in taking on Norton. His position was quite different from Ripley's. He was that *rara avis* in Boston in the 1830's: a full-fledged rationalist. He was amused to see Norton defending miracles as zealously as an old-fashioned Calvinist defended the Trinity and at the same time attempting to ground his theology on the sensational psychology of Locke. Hildreth did not pretend to share Ripley's or Emerson's belief in intuitive perceptions, but he did point out to Norton that without some such belief the case for religion was shaky indeed. For, he said, a real empiricist, confronted with a miracle, would never take it as a sign that the performer possessed supernatural authority; he would begin looking at once for natural explanations for such an unusual happening. In rejecting the concept of religious feeling, therefore, Norton, said Hildreth, was exposing religion "on the open plain, bare and unsheltered, to the sharp daggers of the understanding." Hildreth thought Norton rested his religion on a broken reed. "To be true to your principles," he told Norton, "to abide the decision of the test to which you appeal, you ought to be an infidel, you ought to be an atheist." Norton took no notice of Hildreth. Instead, he sought help from the Calvinists; in reprinting his exchange with Ripley he appended two articles attacking Emerson taken from the orthodox *Princeton Review*. Better a halfway house to Calvinism than to "transcendentalism, infidelity, and pantheism"!

Theodore Parker, a minister in West Roxbury who had just turned thirty, had been following the miracles controversy with zest from the beginning and he eventually decided to get in on the action. He thought

Emerson's address "the noblest and most inspiring strain I ever listened to," and he was amused by its repercussions. "It is thought that chaos is coming back," he told a friend, and that the world was coming to an end. "For my part," he added, "I see that the sun still shines, the rain rains, and the dogs bark, and I have great doubts whether Emerson will overthrow Christianity at this time." Parker was not impressed by Norton's assault on Emerson. "Isn't it the weakest thing you ever fancied?" he exclaimed to Elizabeth Peabody. "What a cumbersome matter he makes Christianity to be." Norton, he said, was "a *born Pope*. He settles questions . . . *ex cathedra*. . . . What hope or inspiration is possible for a man looking everlastingly back?" Parker approved of Ripley's initial response to Norton, though Ripley didn't say "all that I wish might be said," but he was disappointed to see the discussion get off into bickering about German theology. "There is a higher word to be said on this subject than Ripley is disposed to say right now," he declared; and he joined battle with Norton early in 1840 with a pamphlet entitled *The Previous Question between Mr. Andrews Norton and His Alumni Moved and Handled in a Letter to All Those Gentlemen*, attributed to "Levi Blodgett," but soon known as Parker's.

Parker's entry into the arena was especially vexatious to Norton and his sympathizers because Parker spelled out in bold detail the implications of the New Views for historical Christianity and because, unlike Emerson and Ripley, he remained in the church. In his Levi Blodgett pamphlet, Parker announced frankly that Christianity was only one among many world religions (though, indeed, "the highest, and even a perfect religion") and that, like all religions, it rested on two fundamental truths: the existence of God and man's sense of dependence on him. But the germs of these truths were innate in human nature, according to Parker, and by searching within oneself any person could grasp them and begin to develop them in all their ramifications. The great distinction of Jesus was that he intuited these primary truths more clearly than anyone before him and lived them out more nobly than anyone else who had ever lived. He may have performed miracles, given his extraordinary benevolence, acknowledged Parker, but these had nothing to do with the validity of the truths which he apprehended. Just as miracles would have added nothing to the truths which Socrates uttered nor to the beauty of the pictures Raphael painted, so the miracles reported in the New Testament added nothing to the spiritual quality of the sentiments voiced by Jesus. At any rate, it was impossible to prove the authenticity of any of these miracles. Nor was it necessary. It was wiser to rest the authority of Christianity not on the person of Jesus but on the eternal nature of the truths he uttered.

Shortly after the appearance of Parker's pamphlet, the Berry Street Conference, a Unitarian clerical association to which Parker belonged, met to discuss the question "Ought differences of opinion on the value and authority of miracles to exclude men from Christian fellowship and sympathy with one another?" The meeting ended inconclusively, but Parker, who sat quietly throughout the proceedings, was upset by the coolness of the members, particularly the older clergy, toward him. Later on he began to run into difficulties arranging pulpit exchanges with other ministers. "This is the nineteenth century!" he wrote sorrowfully in his journal. "This is Boston! This among the Unitarians!" But his determination to set his fellow Unitarians straight on matters of religion remained firm. Invited to deliver the ordination sermon for a young minister in South Boston in May, 1841, he chose as his topic: "A Discourse of the Transient and Permanent in Christianity." He took his title from an essay by David Strauss, whose *Life of Jesus*, published in

Germany in 1835, was regarded as outlandish by liberal as well as orthodox Christians in the United States at this time. The theme of Parker's sermon was extremely simple: Christian forms, rites, creeds, doctrines, theology, even the church itself, were transitory; only the great truths intuited by Jesus had enduring value for the human race. Parker made no secret of his negations. The infallible inspiration of both Old and New Testaments went quickly by the board. So did the personal authority of Jesus. ("It is hard to see why the great truths of Christianity rest on the personal authority of Jesus, more than the axioms of geometry rest on the personal authority of Euclid or Archimedes.") Even if Jesus had never lived, said Parker, the truths he taught would stand firm, though, of course, the world would have lost the example of his beautiful character.

> Measure him by the world's greatest sons—how poor they are! Try him by the best of men—how little and low they appear! Exalt him as much as we may, we shall yet perhaps come short of the mark. But still was he not our brother; the son of man, as we are; the son of God, like ourselves? His excellence—was it not human excellence? His wisdom, love, piety,—sweet and celestial as they were,—are they not what we also may attain?

Christianity for Parker was "absolute, pure morality; absolute, pure religion,—the love of man; the love of God acting without let or hindrance." Its only command was: "Thou shalt love the Lord thy God with all thy heart, and with all thy soul, and with all thy mind; thou shalt love thy neighbor as thyself." And from this command came the duties enjoined by Jesus: humility, reverence, sobriety, gentleness, charity, forgiveness, fortitude, resignation, faith, and active love. The Christianity of sects, of the pulpit, and of society was ephemeral, said Parker, but the truths intuited by Jesus were perennial.

The uproar over Parker's ordination sermon was, if anything, even greater than that over Emerson's Divinity School Address. Three clergymen of different denominations united in making a formal protest against the sermon and another minister called on Massachusetts authorities to send Parker to prison for blasphemy. Some ministers cut him dead when they met him on the street and all but a handful refused to allow him in their pulpits. "As far as the ministers are concerned," lamented Parker, "I am *alone*, ALL ALONE." But his West Roxbury congregation stood by him and he continued his crusade for what he regarded as true religion despite all the outcries of "unbeliever," "blasphemer," "infidel," and "atheist" that raged about him.

In the winter of 1841-42, Parker gave further offense in a series of lectures in Boston (published as *A Discourse of Matters Pertaining to Religion* in 1842), in which he announced: "If Christianity be true at all, it would be just as true if Herod or Catiline had taught it." He gave more offense in October, 1842, when he called the action of the Hollis Street Council in forcing an outspoken Unitarian minister to resign a "piece of diplomacy worthy of a College of Jesuits." He compounded his offenses in a lecture in Boston on December 26, 1844, in which he not only suggested the possibility that Jesus might have taught some errors along with his great truths, but also said that the God who inspired Jesus might have additional and even greater Christs in store for humankind. (One minister friendly to Parker drew the line at this point: ". . . when you talk about future Christs, I can't bear ye.")

By this time the Boston Association of Unitarian ministers had held a special meeting with Parker (January, 1843), hoping to persuade him to resign. "He that rejects

the Church must not belong to it," declared Nathaniel
Frothingham of the First Church in Boston. "If one
wishes to throw stones at the windows, he must go outside." But Parker refused to go outside and the Association drew back from expelling him. Still, he remained a
virtual pariah in the Unitarian community. A Unitarian
layman wrote the Boston *Courier* to say: "I would rather
see every Unitarian congregation in our land dissolved
and every one of our churches occupied by other denominations or razed to the ground than to assist in
placing a man entertaining the sentiments of Theodore
Parker in one of our pulpits." When the Reverend John
Sargent exchanged pulpits with Parker in November,
1844, he was dismissed from his church. In December,
1844, after Parker delivered the "Great and Thursday
Lecture" on the relation of Jesus to his age at the First
Church in Boston, the Boston Association took immediate action to ensure that he never lectured there
again. And in January, 1845, when James F. Clarke
exchanged pulpits with him, several members of Clarke's
church resigned in protest.

In the end, however, a group of Unitarian laymen,
determined that Parker "shall have a chance to be heard
in Boston," organized the Twenty-eighth Con-
gregational Society, secured Melodeon Hall on Washing-
ton Street, and invited Parker to become minister. At his
formal installation in January, 1846, he gave the sermon,
"The True Idea of a Christian Church," in which he
viewed the church as a society for promoting good
works. In the years that followed, people flocked to hear
his provocative sermons, and though the pulpits of Boston were closed to him he soon had the largest parish in
Boston, if not in the nation, and he became known as "the
Great American Preacher."

By the time the miracles controversy subsided, there
were many respectable New Englanders who had come

to regard Transcendentalism with horror and loathing. "A transcendentalist, sir, is an enemy to the institution of Christianity," thundered one Unitarian minister. His opinion was not uncommon. After the Divinity School Address, Emerson was not invited to speak at Harvard again for nearly thirty years. As for Parker, when he was in his last illness in Italy in 1859, the Boston Association turned down a resolution to express sympathy for him in his suffering. "We preach authoritative miracle-sanctioned Christianity," said one Unitarian firmly. "How can we unite in teaching with him who abjures all this. . . ?" Long before his death Parker was being referred to in the Unitarian press as a "lecturer . . . formerly recognized as a Unitarian preacher."

Transcendentalism and Unitarianism

Still, the rift between Transcendentalists and Unitarians was by no means absolute. Some Unitarians followed the development of the New Views with sympathetic interest and had cordial relations with their exponents. William Ellery Channing expressed enough interest in the New Views to be suspected (by Norton, for one) of being something of a Transcendentalist himself. Actually he was not. He continued to believe firmly in the historicity of the New Testament miracles and in the personality of God, and he looked askance at the Transcendental belief in the primacy of private inspiration and deprecated the tendency toward pantheism. "The danger that besets our Transcendentalists," he told Elizabeth Peabody, "is that they sometimes mistake their individualities for the Transcendent," thus falling into a kind of "*ego-theism*." At the same time he was anxious for the Unitarians not to develop an orthodoxy of their own and he warmly supported free inquiry in all religious matters. "This Unitarianism which so many people think is the last word. . . ," he declared, "is only the vestibule." Channing feared that Unitarianism was becoming conventional and stationary and was repelling bright and lively young minds, and he followed all new developments in religion with eager and hopeful interest. Emerson's Divinity School Address he regarded as "an entirely justifiable and needed criticism on the perfunctory character of service creeping over the Unitarian churches," though he was bothered by its indifference to the New Testament miracles and its seeming rejection of the personality of God. He took a similar attitude toward Parker's South Boston sermon. Though disturbed by Parker's rejection of Jesus' miracles, he liked his emphasis on the immutableness of Christian truth, said he wished Parker would continue to "preach what he thoroughly feels and believes," and refused to desert him during the commotion that followed the sermon. But he told Elizabeth Peabody: ". . . I get no light from the 'new views.' I seem to *learn* very little. Their vague generalizations do not satisfy me." Still, his relations with Transcendentalists like Emerson, Ripley, and Parker remained amicable until his death in 1842, and he followed their activities closely. Emerson called Channing "our Bishop," Ripley described himself as "a child of Channing," Alcott gave him first place in a list of people who apprehended the spiritual ideal, and Parker regarded him as a "great man—and a good man."

Like Channing, James Walker, editor of the *Christian Examiner* from 1831 to 1839, took a friendly interest in Transcendentalism, accepted essays by Ripley and other young writers for publication, and refused to share Norton's alarm over the New Views. Without in any serious sense espousing the Newness himself, he nevertheless recognized the claims of intuition, praised Schleiermacher and DeWette, and, above all, reminded his colleagues at Harvard that if they wanted to put down

Transcendentalism, "they must first deign to comprehend its principles." Even more sympathetic to the New Views than Channing or Walker was William Henry Furness, Philadelphia minister with close associations in Boston. In *Remarks on the Four Gospels* (1836), Furness stressed direct intuition of religious truth rather than miracles and, while accepting the historicity of the New Testament, blended material and spiritual realms in such a way as to absorb miracles (which he claimed Jesus did perform) into the natural world. "Natural facts become supernatural," he declared, "and miracles become natural, when all are regarded as manifestations of an Invisible Mind, an Infinite Will." There was enough obscurity in his position to keep him out of trouble with the orthodox; and during the furor over Emerson's Divinity School Address he assured Norton of his orthodoxy.

Among the older generation of Unitarian clergymen, perhaps only Convers Francis could be considered something of a Transcendentalist. "You have the highest peaks of your mind at least a little gilded with transcendentalism," his sister told him. Pastor of the First Church in Watertown, Massachusetts, Francis was on good terms with Emerson and Parker, attended meetings of the Transcendental Club as a kind of elder statesman, published a pamphlet entitled *Christianity as a Purely Internal System* (1836), which seemed to align him with the Newness, and professed regard for Emerson even after the Divinity School Address. But when the crunch came —his friend Parker came under fire just as Francis was about to receive an appointment at Harvard—he retreated into silence. Parker promised not to embarrass him by continuing their association, but to his journal he lamented: "Francis fell back on account of his Professorship at Cambridge!"

Among the younger Unitarian clergymen, Transcendentalism did considerably better. At least two ministers—Frederic Henry Hedge and James Freeman Clarke—regarded themselves as both Christians and Transcendentalists. Hedge, who had studied in Germany as well as at Harvard and who had a church in Maine, was one of the few Transcendentalists who could read German philosophy and theology in the original. In an influential series of articles for the *Christian Examiner* in the early 1830's, he presented an excellent exposition of modern German thought and used the term "Transcendentalism" for the first time in the sense in which it was to become important in New England. At meetings of the Transcendental Club he helped familiarize his friends with the new German ideas. "Germanicus" Hedge didn't accept Emerson's views on revelation; he wanted to combine Christian supernaturalism with the Transcendental emphasis on intuition. "What religion wants and declares," he said, "is a Father in Heaven, a moral governor and judge of the rational world. Of this God the natural proofs are our own consciousness, our moral instincts, and the universal account of mankind." Though Hedge didn't think miracles were essential to the Christian faith, he thought they were "historically true" and he also believed in the divinity of Christ.

James F. Clarke was also a Christian Transcendentalist. Like Hedge, he lived outside of Boston during the early days of Transcendentalism. His pastorate was in Louisville, Kentucky, where he edited a monthly, the *Western Messenger*, which was receptive to the New Views. Clarke professed sympathy with what he called the "new school." There was, he pointed out in 1838,

a large and increasing number of the clergy and laity, of thinking men and educated women, especially of the youth in our different colleges, of all sects and all professions, who are dissatisfied with

the present state of religion, philosophy, and literature. The common principle which binds them together and makes them if you choose a school, is a
desire for more of LIFE, soul, energy, originality in
these great departments of thought.

Clarke was an intuitionalist and he reviewed Emerson's
Divinity School Address favorably in the *Western
Messenger*, stoutly denying that Emerson was an infidel,
pantheist, atheist, or non-Christian. When faculty control over student speakers at the Divinity School was
proposed, he exclaimed sarcastically: "This is indeed a
'New View,'" and asked whether Harvard Unitarians
were planning to adopt the "religious exclusiveness" of
their erstwhile Calvinist foes. In 1841, Clarke returned
to his native Boston and established the Church of the
Disciples (sometimes called the "transcendental church")
and when Parker got into trouble he offered him a place
to preach and lost several church members for doing so.
"I am a Transcendentalist," he once announced. "I do
not believe that man's senses tell him all he knows."
Nevertheless, he believed that Christianity rested on the
messianic claims of Jesus, and he disagreed with the
Transcendentalists' opposition to miracles and to their
"unreasonable denial of the supernatural element in history."

Transcendentalism and Christianity

If Unitarians were by no means of one mind about the
New Views, the Transcendentalists were themselves in
little accord on religion, except for their common belief
in intuitive perception of spiritual truth. There was great
diversity of opinion among leading Transcendentalists
as regards Christianity. Clarke called Parker "the expounder of a Negative Transcendentalism," to contrast

him with Emerson, "the expounder of a Positive Transcendentalism," probably because of the former's emphatic way of putting things. In point of fact, Emerson's negations when it came to Christianity were more far-ranging than even Parker's. By generalizing miracles to cover all natural processes and by internalizing revelation in the hearts of all men and women, Emerson pulled the props out from under historical Christianity. Nor was his view of God as impersonal force (which Parker did not share) any less subversive of traditional Christian views, as both Norton and Ware fully recognized. A few months before the Divinity School Address, Emerson wrote in his journal:

> What shall I answer to these friendly youths who ask of me an account of theism, and think the views I have expressed of the impersonality of God desolating and ghastly? I say that I cannot find, when I explore my own consciousness, any truth in saying that God is a person, but the reverse. I feel that there is some profanation in saying he is personal. To represent him as an individual is to shut him out of my conscience.

Emerson, unlike Parker, felt conscientiously obliged to leave the church. "I have sometimes thought," he reflected, "that to be a good minister it was necessary to leave the ministry." He preached intermittently for a number of years thereafter and then quit preaching entirely. (Once, reading a passage from an old sermon, he suddenly paused and exclaimed: "The passage which I have just read *I do not believe*. . . .") Though he never ceased to admire Jesus as a moral leader, he did, on at least one occasion, echo Voltaire's exasperation at hearing the name of Jesus uttered so often. In his journal for 1835, he reflected at length on the character of Jesus:

You affirm that the moral development contains all the intellectual, and that Jesus was the perfect man. I bow in reverence unfeigned before that benign man. I know more, hope more, am more, because he has lived. But, if you tell me that in your opinion he has fulfilled all the conditions of man's existence, carried out to the utmost, at least by implication, all man's powers, I suspend my assent. I do not see in him cheerfulness: I do not see in him love of natural science: I see in him no kindness for art; I see in him nothing of Socrates, of Laplace, of Shakespear. The perfect man should remind us of all great men. Do you ask me if I would rather resemble Jesus than any other man? If I should say Yes, I should suspect myself of superstition.

Parker esteemed Jesus more highly than Emerson; he held him up as the supreme example of wisdom and goodness to follow. In most other respects, though, his views were like Emerson's when it came to religious intuition, the divinity of man, and the miracle of creation. Yet he remained in the church, dedicated it to moral and social reform, and to the end insisted on the personality of God.

Jesus probably meant more to Bronson Alcott than to any other Transcendentalist. Alcott, a Connecticut schoolmaster with an Episcopalian background who came to Boston in 1828 and soon discovered he was a Transcendentalist, thought of Jesus almost as a living person—friend, brother, companion—and was likely to drop his name into just about any conversation he was having. He regarded Jesus as the most skillful teacher who had ever lived and thought his insights into human nature, his spiritual goals, and his pedagogical techniques unsurpassed. Alcott shared Emerson's views on miracles and inspiration, but he was repelled by his impersonal view of Deity. God for Alcott was a "Divine Person" who created and sustained the universe and also dwelt within the hearts of people as "the great inward Commander." Alcott "defended his thesis of personality last night," Emerson once wrote in his journal, "but it is not quite a satisfactory use of words. . . . I see profound need of distinguishing the First Cause as superpersonal. It deluges us with power; we are filled with it; but there are skies of immensity between it and us." George Ripley joined Alcott in taking issue with Emerson's superpersonal view of God and he also shared Alcott's high estimate of Jesus as a moral teacher. Margaret Fuller tended toward theism, like Ripley, Alcott, and Parker, and her view of Jesus was equally exalted. Still, in a "Credo" she composed in 1842, she looked forward to a new ideal for humanity. "We want a life more complete and various than that of Christ," she wrote. "We have had a Messiah to teach and reconcile; let us now have a Man to live out all the symbolical forms of human life, with the calm beauty of a Greek God, with the deep consciousness of a Moses, with the holy love and purity of Jesus."

Some of the Transcendentalists thought Emerson's view of religion was focused too much on the individual believer. Ripley, like Parker, stressed the social side of religion in a way Emerson never did. Ripley believed the purpose of Christianity was to redeem society as well as the individual from sin, and after resigning his pastorate he went off to organize an experimental community at Brook Farm. William Henry Channing, nephew of William Ellery Channing, was another Transcendentalist with an acute social conscience. Convinced that Emerson wasn't sensitive to "the great social idea of our era," Channing founded a church for workers in New York City in 1836 and experimented with several independent churches dedicated to social reform in New York and

Boston before settling down to a regular Unitarian pastorate in Rochester, New York.

Perhaps the most socially active of all the Transcendentalists in the 1830's was Orestes Brownson, an ex-Presbyterian who had tried agnosticism and Universalism before becoming a Unitarian and a Transcendentalist. In his *New Views of Christianity, Society, and the Church* (1836), Brownson proposed that a kind of transcendentalized Unitarianism, uniting "spiritual" Christianity with "material" social reform, could bring about the Kingdom of God on earth. Brownson was rather conservative theologically and thought Emerson too severe with historical Christianity in his Divinity School Address, though he came to his defense after Norton's attack. But Brownson went through his anticlerical stage, too, and in an essay published in 1840 called for the abolition of the "priesthood" as indispensable for social salvation. About this time, however, he was renewing his interest in traditional Christian forms and doctrines, and in 1844 he joined the Catholic church.

Henry David Thoreau was doubtless the most anticlerical of them all. Though he believed in a "Universal Intelligence" and called Jesus "the prince of Reformers and Radicals," his journals are filled with cracks at the Christian church. He preferred the sound of cow bells on Sunday, he wrote, to that of church bells. Another time he noted that he had lectured in the basement of an orthodox church "and I trust helped to undermine it." The church, he wrote, is always the ugliest building in any village, because

it is the one in which human nature stoops the lowest and is most disgraced. Certainly, such temples as these shall ere long cease to deform the landscape. There are few things more disheartening and disgusting than when you are walking the streets of a strange village on the Sabbath, to hear a preacher shouting like a boatswain in a gale of wind, and thus harshly profaning the quiet atmosphere of the day.

In *A Week on the Concord and Merrimack Rivers* (1849), Thoreau included a long passage on Christianity which upset even George Ripley by its unrestrained freethinking. In it, he castigated Christians for their bigotry and intolerance, placed Buddha beside Jesus as a worthy moral teacher, and expressed a preference for the Hindu, Chinese, and Persian religious writings over the Christian Scriptures. He did, however, cite antimaterialistic passages from the New Testament with ironic approval and exclaim: "Let but one of these sentences be rightly read, from any pulpit in the land, and there would not be left one stone of that meeting-house upon another." But the New Testament, he added, treated of man's spiritual affairs too exclusively, and Jesus, though "a sublime actor on the stage of the world," taught mankind "but imperfectly how to live" since his thoughts were all directed toward another world. Thoreau, like Emerson, rejected belief in personal immortality, though both of them thought of the individual as part of a life process that was eternal. Most of the other Transcendentalists—Parker and Margaret Fuller, for example—believed in personal immortality. Jones Very, Transcendentalist poet, even announced he was a believer in the resurrection of the body, leading Dr. George B. Loring to exclaim: "I would not be, if I had his body." But Thoreau insisted there was "no heaven but that which lies about me" and he also had the impression that people who clung tenaciously to the Biblical miracles did so because there was no real miracle in their own lives. "A healthy man," he explained, with steady employment, as wood-chopping at fifty cents a cord, and a camp in the woods, will not be a good subject for Christianity. The New Testament may be a choice book to him on some, but not on all or most of his days. He will rather go a-fishing in his leisure hours.

Christianity "has dreamed a sad dream," Thoreau concluded, "and does not yet welcome the morning with joy." It dwelt on human imperfections, overemphasized the sickly conscience, and stressed repentance rather than reflection. Thoreau agreed with Emerson in thinking the Christian church was immersed in verbal formulas and remote from the substance of daily living. "What is religion?" Thoreau once asked. "That which is never spoken."

Emerson for his part mellowed some in later years. He began attending church occasionally toward the end of his life and even came to favor compulsory chapel for Harvard undergraduates after the Civil War. Yet he was also present at the founding of the Free Religious Association, an organization of freethinkers, in 1867, and delivered an address to its members that made it clear he had not abandoned any of the views he had first set forth in the Divinity School Address of 1838. To rationalists, secularists, and freethinkers in the late nineteenth century, in Britain as well as America, he continued to be a hero because of his critique of historical Christianity. And the Unitarian church in the United States gradually went over to his views and even beyond after his death in 1882.

Still, Emerson, like Thoreau, regarded himself as basically religious. In his last public address, to some Harvard divinity students, he exclaimed: ". . . unlovely, nay, frightful, is the solitude of the soul which is without God

in the world." According to his son, he always expected
Sunday to be observed in the household in some way:
reading, reflecting, walking in the woods, conversing
with a close friend, or even listening to a minister in
church. One Sunday he asked a woman who was working
in the house whether she had been to church and when
she said, No, she didn't trouble the church much, Emerson said quietly, "Then you have somewhere a little
chapel of your own." As for Thoreau:

> I see, smell, taste, hear, feel that everlasting Some-
> thing to which we are allied, at once our maker, our
> abode, our destiny, our very Selves; the one historic
> truth, the most remarkable fact which can become
> the distinct and uninvited subject of our thought,
> the actual glory of the universe; the only fact which a
> human being cannot avoid recognizing, or in some
> way forget or dispense with.

In its sense of joy and wonder at creation and in its
deep-seated belief that natural processes possessed un-
mistakable direction and purpose, American Transcendentalism, for all its heresies, was profoundly religious in
temper. The philosophy which the Transcendentalists
worked out as they developed the New Views was essentially an appendage to their religious affirmations. No
matter how much they philosophized, they never lost
their feeling of awe and reverence toward the universe.
" 'Miracles are ceased!' " Emerson reflected in 1837.

> Have they indeed? When? They had not ceased this
> afternoon when I walked into the wood and got into
> bright, miraculous sunshine, in shelter from the
> roaring wind. Who sees a pine-cone or the turpen-
> tine exuding from the tree, or a leaf, the unit of
> vegetation, fall from its bough, as if it said, "the year

is finished," or hears in the quiet, piny glen the chickadee chirping his cheerful note, or walks along the lofty promontory-ridges which, like natural causeways, traverse the morass, or gazes upward at the rushing clouds, or downward at a moss or a stone and says to himself, "Miracles have ceased?"

CHAPTER TWO

Intuitional Philosophy

TRANSCENDENTALISM was originally a derisive term in New England. "I was given to understand," wrote Charles Dickens after visiting the region, "that whatever was unintelligible would be certainly transcendental." Like so many other pejorative terms, however, the expression "Transcendentalism" came in time to be accepted with pleasure and pride by its exponents. The ideas it designated were also known as the Newness, the New Views, the New School, the Intuitional Philosophy, and the Movement, and there were almost as many attempts at precise definitions as there were Transcendentalists. But those who wanted to be mystified by it—Harvard's Andrews Norton and Francis Bowen and Yale's Noah Porter—continued to be mystified by it all.

Emerson once suggested that if a person wished to know what Transcendentalism was he should empty his mind of everything coming from tradition and the rest would be Transcendentalism. Orestes Brownson defined Transcendentalism as "the recognition in man of the capacity of knowing truth intuitively, or of attaining to a scientific knowledge of an order of existence transcending the reach of the senses"; George A. Ripley said its leading idea was "the supremacy of mind over matter"; William H. Channing called it "an assertion of the inalienable integrity of man, of the immanence of Divinity in instinct"; Theodore Parker identified it with the doctrine that man has "faculties which give him ideas and intuitions which transcend sense experience"; and Christopher Cranch told his disapproving father that it was a "synonym for one who, in whatever way, preaches the spirit rather than the letter." But perhaps Emerson, in his lecture "The Transcendentalist," gave the best explanation of what the word meant:

> What is popularly called Transcendentalism among us, is Idealism; Idealism as it appears in 1842.... It is well known to most of my audience that the Idealism of the present day acquired the name Transcendental from the use of that term by Immanuel Kant, of Königsberg, who replied to the skeptical philosophy of Locke, which insisted that there was nothing in the intellect which was not previously in the experience of the senses, by showing that there was a very important class of ideas or imperative forms, which did not come by experience, but through which experience was acquired; that these were intuitions of the mind itself; and he denominated them *Transcendental* forms. The extraordinary profoundness and precision of that man's thinking have given vogue to his nomenclature, in Europe and America, to that extent that whatever belongs to the class of intuitive thought is popularly called at the present day *Transcendental*.

Kant, in short, was the fountainhead of American Transcendentalism. Most Transcendentalists did not, to be sure, tackle Kant in the original; they learned about him secondhand, mainly through the English Romantics Samuel Taylor Coleridge and Thomas Carlyle. Nor did most of them, Emerson included, have an accurate grasp at all points of what Kant was saying; they made general use of him, as they did of other philosophers, for their own purposes. Still, Kant cast his light over the entire Transcendental movement in New England. His critique of British empiricism was enormously helpful to young men and women who were beginning to find the philosophy of John Locke, which had been their birthright, painfully unsatisfying. His moral philosophy, presented without any theological trappings, was also tremendously appealing to people who were struggling to free themselves from the Puritan tradition without throwing aside its moral impulse. The Kantian philosophy in its broadest aspects, in other words, met the deep-seated needs of young, educated middle-class Americans in New England (and eventually in other parts of the country) in the first part of the nineteenth century, and made Transcendentalists out of many of them. But the young Transcendentalists blended what they learned from Kant with ideas coming from other sources and with those springing from the actions and passions of their own time and place. Ripley hailed Kant for the light he had thrown on the great questions of human existence; Parker said that Kant, "one of the profoundest thinkers in the world, though one of the worst writers, even of Germany," had given him "the true method, and put me on the right road"; and even Alcott, for whom sustained reasoning of any kind was distasteful, copied fifty-seven pages from a book on Kant into his journal.

Kantian Idealism

It was David Hume, Kant once said, who had

awakened him from his dogmatic slumber, though Kant in fact was neither dogmatic in temper nor ever unaware of the major philosophical issues of his day. But he was especially bothered by Hume's contention that for a Lockean empiricist there was no objective basis in reality for such abstract ideas as causality. Locke's empiricism held that the human mind was a *tabula rasa*, a blank tablet, which passively received sense impressions from the outer world and combined them by mechanical laws of association into complex ideas. But if this were so, Hume argued, we could never know what "cause" is; we perceive sequences of sense impressions (temporal succession) but we never perceive causal relations among them (causal succession). What seems causal to us is merely customary; we're used to observing one particular event followed by another particular event and conclude, unjustifiably, that it will always happen that way. (Hume also called into question the existence of God, the soul, and the external world by the same line of empirical reasoning, thus putting religion and philosophy, as well as science, on the defensive.) Hume's analysis, Kant recognized, undercut the very foundation of Newtonian science ("Every event," Newton had said, "has a cause"), and he felt obliged as a philosopher who did scientific work as well to reestablish the validity of causality as a universal and necessary relation on which modern science might rest. He was also concerned to find a basis for mathematical relations in experience and, in addition, to explore the relation between scientific and moral knowledge, for he thought moral experience yielded even deeper truths about reality than science did. Kant's major ideas appeared in two epoch-making treatises, *Critique of Pure Reason* (1781) and *Critique of Practical Reason* (1788), with which all American Transcendentalists had some familiarity, even if only secondhand.

In the *Critique of Pure Reason*, Kant denied that the

mind was a *tabula rasa*; it was, on the contrary, an active, dynamic organ which crucially shapes our experience of reality. By its very structure, Kant said, the mind imposes certain forms on the raw material coming to it through the senses from the outer world, and our knowledge is thus inescapably in part ideal (shaped by the mind) and in part empirical (produced by the senses). Kant made a tripartite division of the mind into Sensibility, Understanding, and Reason. The Sensibility, he said, intuits (has an immediate awareness of) the material of the external world and in the very act of intuition imposes a spatial and temporal structure upon it. Time and space are not things, for they have no beginning or end; they are intuitions or forms of perception, and the Sensibility, by applying these forms, molds the chaos of sensations it encounters into spatial and temporal sense-images. These spatial and temporal forms are necessary parts of all sense experience; and mathematics, which rests on time and space, had for Kant a solid basis in experience.

Where the Sensibility, with its intuitive forms of space and time, transforms raw sense data into concrete perceptions (objects in space and time), the Understanding, with its "categories of thought," transforms concrete perceptions into abstract conceptions. There were twelve categories of thought, according to Kant, but the most important was the category of causality. Hume was right, Kant thought, in insisting that causality did not inhere in sense experience, but he was wrong in denying its reality. Causality was real enough; it was one of the basic categories of thought which the Understanding imposed on all of the perceptions coming to it from the Sensibility. Causality for Kant was a universal and necessary form of thought transcending sense experience. Just as Sensibility linked all sense data impinging on the mind into spatial and temporal relations, so the Understanding automatically joined all perceptions into causal sequences. Time, space, and causality were thus imbedded in the very structure of the mind; we could not experience reality apart from them. And this is why we cannot think of a beginning or end to time and space and cannot imagine a first cause which is not the effect of a prior cause.

What is the external world, the thing-in-itself, really like apart from our spatial, temporal, and causal grasp of it? Human reason, said Kant, inevitably seeks to know what ultimate reality is; it tries to unify the concepts provided by the Understanding in order to produce metaphysical or religious ideas which will explain the universe as a whole in its fundamental character. But Pure Reason (Kant's term for speculative or theoretical Reason) is doomed to failure, for it works only with concepts and never with objects of experience. Pure Reason may analyze, clarify, unify, and systematize the concepts belonging to the Understanding, but it must never assume that there is anything in objective experience corresponding to the ideas which it produces in the course of ratiocination. The Sensibility spatializes and temporalizes sense experience and the Understanding conceptualizes it; but Pure Reason does not operate on experience and it can never achieve any real knowledge of the objective universe apart from the patterns which the Sensibility and the Understanding impose on it. The ideas of Pure Reason may be useful in bringing order and unity into our thinking at the highest level of abstraction, but they are "regulative" of our thinking only, not "constitutive" of it (as the categories of Understanding are), and there is nothing in experience corresponding to them. Pure Reason, in short, can never prove the truth of such religious and moral ideas as God, freedom, and immortality. On the other hand, Practical Reason (Kant's term for Reason functioning in the realm of action) could, Kant believed, find a valid basis for accepting these ideas as necessary postulates for our moral life.

In his *Critique of Practical Reason*, Kant held that morality is reason in action and he outlined the conduct which he thought was required of people as rational beings. Man, he said, was a moral being who had the duty to follow the moral law prescribed by his reason. Like the forms of sensible intuition and the categories of Understanding, the moral law is *a priori*, that is, universal and necessary and prior to (not derived from) experience. In formulating the moral law, then, our Practical Reason lays down unconditional commands (or categorical imperatives) for us to follow in our relations with one another, regardless of time and place: (1) Act only in conformity with that maxim which you can at the same time will to be a universal law; (2) Act in such a way as to use humanity, whether in your own person or in the person of another, always as an end and never merely as a means; and (3) Act as if, through your maxim, you were always a lawmaking member in a universal kingdom of ends. Failure to act on these universal moral principles discovered by Practical Reason breeds ill will, suspicion, and distrust, Kant observed, and it vitiates social relations; willingness to be guided by them strengthens the mutual faith and trust on which all social life depends and advances us toward the ideal community of rational beings, which should be our highest moral goal. By behaving, in fact, as if we already belong to this ideal community, Kant thought, we help to bring it about. But Kant was not really sanguine about the ability of human beings to live by these formulations of the categorical imperative with any great success. Our inclinations and desires, he recognized, are perpetually at war with our sense of duty and we are continually tempted to act from prudence, pleasure, and profit rather than from moral principle.

The struggle between duty and desire, Kant thought,

was ceaseless in all human beings and it is always painfully difficult to try to act from principle. To give point to our moral efforts, then, we must make three fundamental assumptions about the nature of things: (1) that we actually have the capacity to act rationally rather than mechanically (freedom); (2) that we have endless time ahead of us in which to carry on the toilsome struggle and that our striving will someday be rewarded (immortality); and (3) that the universe is so designed as to make our moral struggle meaningful (God). Kant, in short, having denied that Pure Reason could establish the validity of God, freedom, and immortality, decided that Practical Reason could assume them as necessary postulates for moral endeavor. He removed reason, Kant once said, to make room for faith; Practical Reason, in other words, could postulate what Pure Reason could not demonstrate. To some extent, moreover, Kant also removed religion to make room for morality, for he replaced the God of Abraham, Isaac, and Jacob with a moral postulate. The American Transcendentalists were impressed by Kant's transcendental idealism (his belief that our experience of the universe is molded by transcendental forms inherent in the mind), but it was his moral philosophy (the emphasis on duty, moral law, and the inferiority of mere utilitarian values) that made the greatest impact on them. They also learned something from idealistic German philosophers (J. G. Fichte and F. W. J. Schelling) and theologians (J. G. Herder, W. M. L. DeWette, and Friedrich Schleiermacher) working along Kantian lines. From Fichtean idealism, Emerson may have derived his definition of the natural world (in *Nature*) as "all NOT-ME" and from Schelling's philosophy of identity (which looked on nature and mind as identical) he probably received reinforcement for his own idealistic view of nature. And from Schleiermacher, Parker learned both to emphasize the autonomy of the religious life and base his belief in God and immortality on feeling or the "religious consciousness." But the overarching influence on American Transcendentalism was Kantianism, though the New Englanders stressed the intuitive rather than the rational elements in Kant's philosophy and hopelessly confused Pure and Practical Reason.

Scottish Common Sense Philosophy

Kantianism was not the only school of thought to emerge in Europe in response to Humean skepticism. What came to be called the Scottish common-sense philosophy or Scottish realism also developed in the late eighteenth and early nineteenth centuries in an effort to refute Hume, and it had a profound effect on American thought, especially in academia, down to the Civil War. Thomas Reid, founder of the school, and his followers (men like Dugald Stewart and Thomas Brown) were eager to retain as much of Locke's empiricism as possible without leaving it exposed to Humean doubts and they did so by positing certain basic judgments of common sense or self-evident principles of reason which they said undergirded all empirical knowledge: belief in the objective existence of the outer world, in personal identity, in causation, and in the uniformity of the laws of nature. As Dugald Stewart put it: ". . . I exist; I am the same person to-day that I was yesterday; the material world has an existence independent of my mind; the general laws of nature will continue in future to operate as uniformly as in time past. . . ." In addition to common sense, there was a moral sense, a kind of intuitive moral faculty which, according to the Scots, grasped distinctions between right and wrong and apprehended various moral axioms that provided the basis for conduct. God had placed both common sense and moral sense in the human mind, the

Scottish philosophers maintained, and He had thus made it possible for man to trust his perceptions and by means of them to apprehend His ways.

The Scottish revision of Locke, which dominated Unitarian thinking when Emerson and Thoreau were undergraduates at Harvard, provided an epistemological basis for science, but it also gave the Unitarians something of an epistemological basis for religion. The major motive, indeed, of Scottish philosophers (and of the Unitarian professors at Harvard who took over their system) was to reconcile natural and revealed religion and to provide a natural, reasonable, common-sense basis for accepting the Christian religion. By clearly separating God from His creation, the Scottish thinkers preserved the orthodox Christian notion of God's transcendence and the necessity for revelation. But revelation, their Unitarian disciples at Harvard thought, harmonized very nicely with empiricism; it was a special kind of empirical evidence for the truths of Christianity, because the miracles by which they were made known to man were perceived at first hand by the Evangelists. The Christian believer, they explained, accepted at second hand the testimony of the Evangelists as to their direct experience of miracles in the same way as he accepted at second hand the firsthand observations of astronomers through the telescope.

To the Transcendentalists, of course, none of this was persuasive; like most people, they accepted at second hand only what they were already prepared to believe. Having rejected Christian miracles, they had no need of the epistemological basis for them so carefully worked out by Unitarian theologians making use of Scottish philosophy. No doubt the Scottish philosophy, especially its concept of an intuitive moral sense, which Emerson and other Transcendentalists learned about in the classroom, played some part in shaping the New Views. But the emphasis on miracles and special revelation as well as the continuing predilection for Lockean empiricism made the common-sense philosophy unpalatable to them. When they broke with Unitarianism, they also discarded Scottish realism and turned to Kantian alternatives (as they conceived them) with relief and gratitude.

Coleridgean Reason and Understanding

Kant's philosophy came to America mainly through the English Romantic poet Samuel Taylor Coleridge. Coleridge, who had studied Kant in Germany (the Königsberger, he said, "took possession of me with a giant's hand") and had also mastered German transcendental idealists like Fichte and Schelling, fancied himself something of a philosopher and theologian as well as a poet and literary critic. After what he called "most intense study," he thoroughly mastered Kant's thought and made a competent exposition of Kantian terminology in several of his books. For Americans, Coleridge's most important book was probably *Aids to Reflection*, which appeared in England in 1825. The bent of *Aids* was moral and religious. Coleridge was a devout Anglican and he was interested in philosophy mainly as a handmaiden to religion. Though he had grasped the technicalities of Kant's *Critique of Pure Reason*, it was the *Critique of Practical Reason* from which he drew most of his own philosophy. In *Aids*, Coleridge presented a compilation of passages from the writings of seventeenth-century British divines (themselves Platonists) accompanied by philosophizing of his own along transcendental lines.

James Marsh, President of the University of Vermont and professor of philosophy there, was the first American to discover the book. The spiritual tone of *Aids* pleased Marsh enormously for he, like Coleridge, was looking for philosophical support for religious faith (in his case Calvinism), which to his mind the prevailing Lockean philosophy failed to furnish. In 1829, Marsh published an American edition of *Aids* prefaced by a long "Preliminary Essay" discussing the new transcendental outlook which is sometimes regarded as the first publication of American Transcendentalism. Marsh's edition of *Aids* was extremely influential; it was read and reread by all the young men and women in America who were on their way to becoming Transcendentalists and it has been called the Old Testament of the American Transcendentalist movement. (Emerson's *Nature*, appearing in 1836, was the New Testament.) Most of the American readers of *Aids* simply ignored the orthodox conclusions of Coleridge and Marsh and went for the idealistic philosophy which it contained.

In his preliminary essay and notes for *Aids*, Marsh placed great emphasis on Coleridge's distinction between Reason and Understanding. He was right in doing this, for by the time Coleridge wrote *Aids* he had made this "momentous distinction," as he called it, basic to his religious philosophy. Coleridge took the distinction from Kant but he gave it a spiritual twist it did not have in Kant. Coleridge knew what he was about; he was anxious, like other post-Kantian thinkers, to develop Kant's thought in new directions. Nevertheless, in writing a popular inspirational book like *Aids*, he wanted to avoid technical explanations and the result was that he blurred the meaning of Kantian terms like Sensibility, Understanding, and Pure and Practical Reason. He also ignored the severe limitations that Kant had placed on Pure Reason's ability to grasp ultimate reality, and he elevated Practical Reason's postulates into "truths of reason." He had a tendency, moreover, to use the term "Reason" without qualifying adjectives (Pure or Practical) and thus gave the impression that Reason was a faculty which could have immediate, intuitive, and sure knowledge of spiritual realities. Marsh concluded from all of this (with hearty approval) that the Understanding was a faculty for dealing with material objects while Reason was a faculty for apprehending spiritual truths. The distinction, false to Kant's intentions, became fundamental in American Transcendentalism. Kant's warnings against a philosophy based mainly on intuition—in which, Kant said, "one has no need to work, but has only to listen to and enjoy the oracle that speaks within itself"—did not reach America at this time.

In presenting *Aids* to the American public, Marsh made a special point of recommending the new transcendental philosophy as an alternative to the "sensational" philosophy then prevailing in American institutions of higher learning. Locke's empiricism, Marsh warned, had "an injurious and dangerous tendency" because of its emphasis on the senses and he thought it possible to develop "a truly spiritual religion" only by opposing Locke. Marsh's criticism came at a time when younger Unitarians found they could no longer accept the union of Lockean and Scottish empiricism with Christian supernaturalism. It was all very well to maintain, as Andrews Norton did, that the New Testament miracles, being an outward testimony to divine revelation, gave an empirical support for the Christian faith, but what if one no longer believed in—or cared anything about—New Testament miracles? And what if, having rejected Christian revelation, one still hungered and thirsted after righteousness? Locke, with or without miracles, seemed to idealistic young people to provide scant support for their spiritual aspirations. The general bent of empiricism seemed to them to be materialism (as Hume and Condillac discovered), for if all our ideas come from sense perception of outer things, how is it possible to know anything but the material world?

Orestes Brownson found Locke's philosophy "altogether unfriendly to religion"; pushed "to its last results," he said, "it would deprive man of all but a merely mechanical life, divest the heart of all emotion, wither the affections, dry up the sentiments, and sink the human race into a frigid skepticism." Bronson Alcott objected to Locke because he "shut the soul up in the cave of the Understanding," and Theodore Parker complained that Locke's "sensational" system "could not legitimate my own religious instincts, nor explain the religious history of mankind." Said James Clarke: "Something within me revolted at all such attempts to explain soul out of sense, deducing mind from matter, or tracing the origin of ideas to nerves, vibrations, and vibratiuncles."

Frederic Hedge, who shared Marsh's dissatisfaction with Locke and the Scottish school, wrote an extended review of the Vermonter's edition of *Aids* for the *Christian Examiner* in March, 1833, in which he praised the book for its "sound and important" ideas. Hedge spent part of his review on Coleridge and part on German metaphysics. As the only American at this time who had read Kant in German, he spoke with some authority on the latter subject. He made it clear that there was no easy way to master German transcendentalism; he doubted, in fact, whether it was possible to grasp Kant, Fichte, and Schelling without possessing to some degree the powers of abstraction which these men possessed. "The works of the transcendental philosophers may be translated word for word," he declared, "but still it will be impossible to get a clear idea of their philosophy unless we raise ourselves at once to the transcendental point of view." In explaining this point of view, Hedge did not emphasize,

as Coleridge and Marsh had, the distinction between
Reason and Understanding. Instead, he called attention
to the notions of "free intuition" and "interior consciousness" which he encountered in the Kantian school.
Echoing Marsh's dissatisfaction with Lockean empiricism, he declared, somewhat loftily and probably with
Unitarians like Norton in mind:

> The disciples of Kant wrote for minds of quite
> another stamp, they wrote for minds that seek with
> faith and hope a solution of questions which that
> philosophy meddles not with, —questions which re-
> late to spirit and form, substance and life, free will
> and fate, God and eternity.

Hedge concluded that Kant and his followers had done
much to "extend the spiritual in man, and the ideal in
nature. . . ." Like Coleridge, Hedge knew his Kant, but
like Coleridge he also bent him to his own wishes.

Emerson called Hedge's essay on *Aids* "a living leaping
Logos" and all the young Unitarian liberals who were on
the road to Transcendentalism read it approvingly.
Hedge not only stimulated them to read *Aids* if they
hadn't done so already, but he also encouraged them to
go on to other works by Coleridge—especially *Biographia
Literaria* (1817) and *The Friend* (1809), the latter, published in the United States with a preface by Marsh in
1831—and even to dip into German philosophy and
theology itself. Coleridge's *Aids* was in some respects a
crystallizing book for many incipient Transcendentalists.
Alcott carefully annotated his copy of the book, said it
formed a new era in his intellectual life by relieving him
of the philosophy of sense, and continued to study it for
many years. "He has a tone a little lower than greatness,"
Emerson wrote his aunt of Coleridge, "but what a living
soul, what a universal knowledge!" Margaret Fuller

wrote appreciatively about the English poet in her journal and expressed the conviction that "the benefits conferred by him on this and future ages are as yet incalculable." Parker, despite reservations about Coleridge's "vanity, prejudice, sophistry, confusion, and opium," agreed with her that Coleridge had done "great service in New England in helping to emancipate enthralled minds." Reading Coleridge, Clarke recalled years later, "I discovered that I was a born Transcendentalist"; Coleridge's writings "confirmed my longing for a higher philosophy than that of John Locke and David Hartley, the metaphysicians most in vogue with the early Unitarians down to the time of Channing." From Coleridge, Elizabeth Peabody recalled, "I first learned the meaning of the word 'transcendental.' "

In addition to supplying young Unitarian rebels with an alternative to the "sensational" philosophy, Coleridge's *Aids* also gave them an epistemology in its distinction between Understanding and Reason. This dichotomy was probably the most important contribution that Coleridge made to American Transcendentalism in its early stages of development. "This distinction," said Clarke, "helped me much in my subsequent studies in theology." It also helped other Transcendentalists who were in the process of thinking their way out of the Unitarian consensus, but perhaps no one more than Emerson. Emerson thought that a clear perception of the different ways in which Understanding and Reason worked was "the key to all theology, and a theory of human life." In a letter written on May 31, 1834, he tried the terms out on his brother Edward:

Philosophy affirms that the outward world is only phenomenal, and the whole concern of dinners, of tailors, of gigs, of balls, whereof men make such account, an intricate dream, the exhalation of the

present state of the soul, wherein the Understanding works incessantly as if it were real, but the eternal Reason, when now and then he is allowed to
speak, declares it is an accident, a smoke, nowise
related to his permanent attributes.

He went on to make explicit what he was talking about:

Now that I have used the words, let me ask you, Do
you draw the distinction of Milton, Coleridge, and
the Germans between Reason and Understanding?
I think it a philosophy itself, and like all truth, very
practical. Reason is the highest faculty of the soul,
what we mean often by the soul itself: it never
reasons, never proves; it simply perceives, it is vision.
The Understanding toils all the time, compares,
contrives, adds, argues; near-sighted but strong-
sighted, dwelling in the present, the expedient, the
customary. Beasts have some understanding but no
Reason. Reason is potentially perfect in every
man—Understanding in very different degrees of
strength. . . . Religion, Poetry, Honor belong to the
Reason; to the real, the absolute. . . .

The distinction between Reason and Understanding
helped shape Emerson's first major publication, *Nature*
(1836), the basic document of American Transcendentalism, which set forth all the major ideas of the new
movement. In *Nature*, Emerson not only presented an
idealistic view of the material world that went far beyond
anything Kant—or even Coleridge—had conceived; he
also analyzed at length the uses of nature to humanity.
After discussing nature as a source of commodities, as a
realm of beauty, and as an inspiration for language,
Emerson turned to the topic of "discipline." Nature, he
said, disciplines both the Understanding and the Reason.

It disciplines the Understanding (the "Hand of the Mind" which "adds, divides, combines, measures") in intellectual truths: the lessons of common sense, the laws of science, and the techniques of agriculture and industry, which give human beings mastery over natural resources. Nature also educates Reason, which operates on a higher level of intellection than the Understanding, by stimulating it to moral, philosophical, and religious insight. Given free rein, according to Emerson, Reason would discover that the natural world has an ethical character and that the moral law "lies at the centre" and "radiates to the circumference." Reason is also able to pierce through the appearance of things to the basic unity underlying all natural phenomena and natural laws—to the "Unity in Variety"—and discover their source in Universal Spirit.

Emerson was neither precise nor consistent in his epistemological terminology. He utilized Coleridge's distinction between Reason and Understanding freely for a number of years after publishing *Nature*, but he also went on using expressions like "moral sentiment," "moral sense," and "sentiment of virtue" (all roughly equivalent), which he had probably learned from the Scottish school at Harvard, as though they were closely related to Coleridgean Reason. By "moral sentiment," Emerson appears to have meant three different things: (1) a kind of sixth sense by which the individual apprehends moral principles (subjective Reason); (2) the moral principles or laws themselves which pervade the universe (objective Reason); and (3) a feeling of warm attachment to these principles. (Corresponding to the "moral sentiment" in its third definition was his expression "religious sentiment," meaning piety or a feeling of love and reverence for the Transcendental deity.) But since Coleridgean Reason was the power or faculty of the mind that has insight into the highest truths, moral and spiritual, about

reality, there was obviously considerable overlapping in
Emerson's thought between Reason and the moral sentiment in its first and third usages. At the same time,
Emerson used another term, "intellect," in a way that
made it equivalent to Coleridge's Understanding. In a
rough way, then, the moral sentiment as ethical insight
corresponded to Reason and the intellect as the power to
generalize from empirical data corresponded to the Understanding in Emerson's thinking.

What was the relation between intellect (Understanding) and moral sentiment (Reason)? Emerson frequently
asserted that they were interdependent. Once the intellect (Understanding) had discovered a scientific truth, he
said repeatedly, the moral sentiment (Reason) must give
joyous assent to it as another glory of the universe, for
otherwise the scientific discovery would go for naught.
Another way of putting it was to say that every scientific
law had moral significance. This meant that intellect
(Understanding) discovered scientific laws and that the
moral sentiment (Reason) interpreted them as moral
laws and that in this fashion the two faculties worked in
harness. But if Emerson sometimes suggested that without the work of intellect (Understanding) there was
nothing for the moral sentiment (Reason) to work on, he
also spoke at other times of Reason's having immediate
intuitions of moral and religious truth without any help
from the Understanding. ("There is no doctrine of
Reason," he said in the Divinity School Address, "which
will bear to be taught by the Understanding.")

Emersonian exegetes have devoted many hours to the
search for consistency in Emerson's use of terms, but
perhaps the only consistency lies in his basic point of
view: ". . . speak what you think today in words as hard as
cannon balls, and tomorrow speak what tomorrow thinks
in hard words again, though it contradict every thing you
said today." The fact is that Emerson never quite made

up his mind (or thought that it was necessary to do so) as to the respective claims of Reason (moral sentiment) and Understanding (intellect), though in the early, heady days of the Transcendental movement he was inclined to give primacy to Reason. But despite his terminological imprecision, he was firm in his belief that intellectual truths have emotional significance: we are filled with peace and joy when we have a new insight in science or mathematics and the appeal of a scientific formula may be aesthetic and moral as well as logical and rational. He was surely wiser than the Harvard Lockeans in his recognition that the mind and heart of man are inseparable and that scientific truth has a moral and aesthetic as well as rational dimension. Twentieth-century physicist Albert Einstein was not exactly a Transcendentalist, but in all his researches into the ultimate constituents of matter he proceeded on moral and aesthetic assumptions: that God was subtle but not malicious and that He expressed Himself with elegant simplicity and majestic consistency.

Theodore Parker did somewhat better with epistemological terms than Emerson. According to Parker, the Understanding supplied material for Reason to ratify or reject. It was important, therefore, to educate the Understanding, that is, to fill it with scientific and historical knowledge (Parker was an omnivorous scholar who knew many languages) so that it could present the facts of the case fairly and accurately to Reason. The "great truths in the Bible did not come by miracles," he once wrote, "but by labour, and watching, and prayers, and tears. . . . This is the way in which inspiration comes." Parker's intuitive belief in God went hand in hand with prodigious research in Biblical scholarship. Emerson, for his part, sometimes shared Parker's view and sometimes did not. He was an industrious scholar himself, but on occasion he simply advised: "Trust your instincts." Yet when young Transcendentalist poet Jones Very showed him some of his pieces and said they had been written under the inspiration of the Holy Spirit, Emerson could not resist asking: "Cannot the spirit parse & spell?" And adding: "We cannot permit the Holy Ghost to be careless and . . . to talk bad grammar." Emerson's friend Thoreau began his career by emphasizing Reason but in his later years his increasing absorption in botanical observations around Concord inclined him toward the Understanding. But Bronson Alcott, sometimes regarded as the most Transcendental of them all, placed Coleridgean Reason above Coleridgean Understanding all of his long life.

The Influence of Carlyle

Coleridge, at any rate, gave American Transcendentalists an epistemology, even if they couldn't always agree on what to do with it. Thomas Carlyle, another vital stimulus during the early days of Transcendental ferment in New England, gave them morale, self-confidence, and the strength of their developing convictions. "We straightway held up our heads" after reading Carlyle, Hedge recalled. Carlyle's first important book, *Sartor Resartus* (1836), appeared in America before it did in England largely through the ministrations of Carlyle's American friend Emerson. Unlike *Aids to Reflection*, which is virtually unreadable today, *Sartor Resartus* ("The Tailor Retailored") remains an engagingly frenetic book. (Emerson, who met both Coleridge and Carlyle when visiting England in 1833 also found Carlyle more congenial.) *Sartor* recounts in vigorous, earthy, and apocalyptic prose the story of Diogenes Teufelsdröck ("God-born Devil's Dung"), who after considerable storm and stress casts aside the mechanical philosophy conceived by his understanding and discovers, through "Pure Reason," his moral autonomy in a deeply spiritual and purposive universe. Carlyle had done a lot of rummaging around in German literature (especially in Goethe and Schiller) and philosophy (Kant and Fichte) and, like Coleridge, he stimulated his American admirers to do some exploring of their own in German thought. Like Coleridge, too, he filled his writings with references to Kantian transcendentalism. Unlike Coleridge, he did not have a good grasp of Kant (he understood Fichte somewhat better), though he pretended he did, and he wreaked havoc with Kantian technicalities. Still, he made his transcendentalism a living, breathing thing and confirmed his American readers in the feeling that they were on the right track.

In *Sartor Resartus*, which Emerson called "a philosophical poem" (and which one young American Transcendentalist always carried around with him), Carlyle made a number of points that appealed to apostles of the New Views in America. He criticized the Lockean tradition, blasted materialism, ridiculed the "Profit-and-Loss Philosophy" of Benthamite utilitarianism, glorified Reason over Understanding, stressed immutable moral law, self-reliance, and the nobility of work, depicted man as a "Soul, a Spirit, and divine Apparition" and the universe as the "living Garment of God," and, in a remarkable chapter on "Natural Supernaturalism," urged people to pierce through mundane appearances and conceive all of nature as a miracle and every phenomenon in it as an incomprehensible wonder. The tone of the book—its blunt candor, moral earnestness, spiritual fervor—also impressed idealistic young Americans. Margaret Fuller hailed Carlyle for teaching "that we must live, and not merely pretend to others that we live," and Emerson said simply: "I love his love of truth." Clarke praised Carlyle for breaking the "evil enchantment" of Locke and creating "a new heaven and a new earth, a new religion and a new life." He thought Carlyle was helping young people to "look at realities instead of names, at substance instead of surface,—to see God in the world, in nature, in life, in providence, in man,—to see divine truth and beauty and wonder everywhere around." Thoreau regarded Carlyle's writings as "a gospel to the young of this generation," and Emerson noted that Carlyle spoke to "youthful minds with an emphasis that hindered them from sleep." Looking back on the 1830's, Ripley wrote many years later that "the transcendental young men and maidens of Boston" found "a new Pentecost" in Carlyle's "wondrous suggestions of a nobler life than the barren routine of custom and tradition." Carlyle's book, he thought,

> . . . formed a new era in the history of mental progress in New England. Solitary students on whom the burden of ancient dogmas pressed heavily rejoiced in the pregnant hints which threw a fresh light on the mysteries of faith and destiny. The enemies of Pharasaism, of conceited respectability, of plausible hypocrisy, were made glad by its stern warfare with shining pretense and insincerity.

Emerson repeatedly urged Carlyle to visit the United States, but without success, and at one time wanted him to edit a journal his American admirers were planning, to be called *The Transcendentalist* or *The Spiritual Inquirer*. Carlyle's influence waned after a few years. He lost interest in transcendentalism (he came to call it "moonshine"), and American Transcendentalists were disenchanted by his increasingly reactionary social views. Still, he and Emerson remained friends to the end, and no Transcendentalist ever denied his energizing influence during the salad days of American Transcendentalism.

* * *

French Eclecticism, Neoplatonism,
and Oriental Thought

German (Kant, Fichte, Schelling) and English (Coleridge and Carlyle) thinkers were the major influences on
the burgeoning Transcendentalist movement in the
1830's but they were not the only ones. Some Transcendentalists learned more from French than from German
or English writers, and others found ancient Greek writers the most illuminating. And there was at least a handful of Transcendentalists who gained sustenance from
the Oriental scriptures. Emerson once said he read for
"lustres," and this was more or less true of all the Transcendentalists. Having developed an "intuitional
Philosophy" that satisfied their needs, they went on to
read largely for confirmation or elaboration of the New
Views in world literature and philosophy. There was no
Transcendentalist, not even Alcott, who stood absolutely by Reason alone; intuition might give the basic
insight but it helped if the Understanding piled up evidence for the New Views from other sources. The New
Views, after all, were universally applicable, like Kant's
categorical imperative, and it should be no matter for
surprise, the Transcendentalists thought, to discover
them in other cultures. Even Jesus, Emerson decided,
was a Kantian man of Pure Reason.

George Ripley and Orestes Brownson were especially
fond of the French Eclectics, though all the Transcendentalists knew something about them. French Eclecticism, a kind of amalgam of Scottish realism and Kantian
idealism, blossomed around 1820 and was mainly the
work of Victor Cousin and Théodore Jouffroy. The
French system included empirical elements but it was
hostile to Locke and distinctly idealistic in tone. Some
American Transcendentalists learned their Kant from

Cousin and Jouffroy rather than from Coleridge or Carlyle (or Kant). Brownson, who published articles on
French idealism, liked the Eclectics because they converted Kant's Reason into a universal and impersonal
Reason which appeared in each individual as intuition or
"spontaneous reason" and through the latter revealed
spiritual truths (such as the existence of God) that could
be regarded as absolutely authoritative. "The genius of
our country," he declared, "is for Eclecticism." Ripley
liked the Eclectics because he preferred their prose style
to the "dry, anatomical spirit" of Kant and thought
Cousin did a better job of demolishing Locke than Coleridge did, and because he believed that the French system had placed "the great truths of the existence of the
Deity, the free agency of man, his immortality, and his
vocation to moral progress as the chief purpose of his
being, on a deep and solid foundation." He translated
and edited Cousin and Jouffroy and devoted to French
thought five volumes of his fourteen-volume magnum
opus *Specimens of Foreign Standard Literature*, which began
appearing in 1838.

Emerson liked the Eclectics for a while, but his
preference all along was for Plato and the Neoplatonists.
"Plato is philosophy and philosophy is Plato," he declared. "Out of Plato come all things that are still written
and debated among men of thought." Emerson probably
studied Plato more carefully than he did just about any
other writer, and he has been called a Platonist. But
Emerson's Plato had a distinct Neoplatonic coloring, for
Thomas Taylor, the British translator on whose work
Emerson depended, had given a Neoplatonic rendering
of Plato's writings. Emerson read Taylor's translations of
the Neoplatonists (Plotinus, Proclus, Porphyry, and
Iamblicus) as well as of Plato, and he accepted their
version of Platonic thought as authoritative. Plotinus,
third-century philosopher and mystic, became one of

Emerson's favorites. There were several ideas in Plotinus that Emerson adopted, with modifications, into his own Transcendentalism: the belief that the flux of nature was an emanation from a spiritual source; the view of evil as absence of spirit and thus negative in nature; the notion that every part and particle of the universe was a microcosm containing all the laws of nature in miniature; and the idea that mystical union with God, the Supreme Unity, was the highest religious experience. From Neoplatonism, which contained Oriental as well as Greek elements, Emerson went on to Asian thought and took with him Thoreau and Alcott and anybody else he could persuade to go along.

Emerson became keenly interested in Indian, Chinese, and Persian literature during the 1840's, but it was the idealistic philosophy of the Hindus that naturally appealed most to him. In the Hindu sacred texts (especially the *Bhagavad-Gita* and the *Upanishads*) which he was reading diligently in the 1840's, Emerson encountered two ideas that were congenial to his mode of thought: the concept of Brahman, the basic impersonal creative energy from which all things in the universe emerged and to which all would ultimately return; and the concept of Maya ("illusions"), the varied, shifting appearances of the phenomenal world through which one must penetrate in order to recognize the fundamental unity that binds everything in creation together. Emerson used these ideas in his poem "Brahma," published in 1857, and although some Americans expressed mystification and composed parodies of it, Indian scholars have regarded it as the most brilliant presentation in brief form of the gist of Hindu philosophy ever made by a Westerner.

Thoreau learned to like Oriental philosophy (especially Indian) as much as Emerson did and he prepared a series of extracts from the "Ethnical Scriptures"

(Chinese, Hindu, and Persian) for *The Dial* in 1843 and 1844. "In the morning," he reported in *Walden*, "I bathe my intellect in the stupendous and cosmogonal philosophy of the Bhagavat-Geeta. . . ." Like Emerson, Thoreau was also attracted to Hindu mysticism (union with Brahman). To a friend he confessed: "To some extent, and at rare intervals, even I am a yogi." In his enthusiasm for Hindu idealism, Emerson once exclaimed: "The East is grand and makes Europe appear the land of trifles." But he didn't mean this seriously. He simply liked philosophical idealism wherever he encountered it: in England, Germany, France, Greece, or India. It was even better if the distinction between Reason and Understanding (or something pretty close to it) turned up in Plato or Plotinus or Plutarch or Bacon or Milton or some other venerable writer. For the "Intuitional Philosophy" was the most cosmopolitan of all philosophies; it found what it was looking for just about everywhere in the world.

The Case for Intuition

The Transcendentalist case for intuitionalism did not go unchallenged. The assault on Locke, like the assault on miracles, roused the wrath of Unitarian and Calvinist alike. Francis Bowen, Harvard moral philosopher, thought that Transcendentalism was "abstruse in its dogma, fantastic in its dress, and foreign in its origin"; Locke, by contrast, was virtually an American citizen and perhaps even a good Harvard Unitarian. Alexander Everett, editor of the *North American Review*, dismissed the New Views as a reversion to "the Platonic visions of the childhood of the race," and the Reverend Frederick Beasley insisted that Locke "never has been and never can be overthrown." Defenders of Locke claimed that the Transcendentalists had completely distorted the

Britisher's outlook. Locke's philosophy did not support materialism, they said; Locke himself was a good Christian and had accepted miracles and divine revelation. Locke's empiricism, moreover, had been a boon to mankind; it had given a boost to science and technology, which in turn had produced mechanical devices for lightening man's labor and releasing much of his time for spiritual pursuits. Locke did not, it was proudly acknowledged, meddle with the "grand secrets" and "mysterious relations" which were such a rage in Transcendental circles; he dealt only with "what can be known" and his inquiries were far more fruitful. "Give us Locke's Mechanism," cried Timothy Walker in the *North American Review*, "and we will envy no man's Mysticism."

Nor did champions of Locke envy the Transcendentalists' epistemology. They simply denied that there was any faculty of the human mind corresponding to Transcendental "Reason." There were two sources of ideas, said the Reverend Leonard Withington, following Locke: sensation and reflection. Sometimes, he explained in the *Quarterly Christian Review* for December, 1834, the mind turned its eye on the outer world, surveyed its operations, learned its laws, and found ways to utilize its powers; and on other occasions the mind looked inward on itself, learned its own powers, and surveyed the agreement or discrepancy among its own ideas. Sensation and reflection; that was the long and short of it, and Withington questioned whether Transcendental Reason was "anything more than a reflexive mind, conscious of its own operations." Withington (and his fellow Lockeans) apparently never doubted whether it was possible to account for the genesis of a Beethoven symphony, a Coleridgean poem ("Kubla Khan"?), or a mathematical theorem on such plain and simple terms. The Transcendental insistence on the limits of conceptual and verbal thinking struck American Lockeans as outrageous. Emerson's belief that there are preconscious and subliminal sources (as we would put it today) for creativity, which sometimes produce sudden flashes of insight, powerful surges of inspiration, and stunning leaps of the imagination, seemed preposterous, even immoral, to Lockeans like Withington. He was so appalled by the Transcendental emphasis on the unconscious and nonrational sources of artistic creativity, scientific discovery, and moral insight that he neglected to mention a third source of ideas for believers like himself: Christian revelation. This was a source that Emerson and his friends could no longer accept, and they found a replacement for it in "Reason" or imaginative insight.

It is easy to fault the Transcendentalists for their untidy epistemology. It is wiser to recognize that the Transcendentalists' view of the mind—with their awareness of the part that unconscious mentation plays in thinking—was fuller, richer, and far more illuminating than the Lockean view with its identification of the mind with conscious thinking. Even Kant recognized that the "dark ideas in man" (that is, the subconscious) were immeasurable and that he had located only a few points on "the great map of our spirit" in his critiques. In his journals, Emerson reported from time to time on the workings of the "Unconscious," as he called it, and he once recorded an experience of having produced some verses with no conscious recollection of how he had done so. Thoreau, like Emerson, was struck by the way ideas sometimes came, "ready-made," into the mind, like flashes of light. Ripley, for his part, was convinced that scientific advance itself depended on the sudden bursts of insight welling up in the consciousness of geniuses like Kepler and Newton. As for Parker, "Truth flashes on the man," he once wrote a friend.

You have felt such visitations; we labour upon a

thought, trying to grasp the truth. We almost have the butterfly in our hands, but cannot get it. Again we try; it will not come; we walk, sit, pray, it will not come. At last in some moment it flashes on us, the crystals form, the work is all done. Whence came it? I do not know. It is in these burning moments that life is lived; the rest is all drudgery, beating the bush, ploughing, and weeding, and watering. This is the harvest hour.

These hours are few to any man, perhaps not more than two in a week; but yet all the real thought of the man is compressed into these burning moments.

Parker, like Emerson, thought the ultimate source for new insights was divine (though he stressed preparatory work on the conscious level); he also regarded these spontaneous intuitions as authoritative. It is not necessary to follow Parker in holding to the divine authority of intuitive insights (the most creative thinkers have had faulty as well as fruitful insights) to recognize that his description of the thinking process was considerably closer to what actually happens than Withington's.

One person's insight is frequently another person's outrage. Withington viewed Transcendental insights as "contemptible nothingism," while the Transcendentalists thought the received wisdom of the day was stifling to the human spirit. The Transcendentalists had alternative moral and religious ideals to offer their age. They were absolutely certain that these ideals were grounded in the very nature of things and that efforts to live by them made for more fruitful and more authentic living than the mechanistic philosophy of the Lockeans.

CHAPTER THREE

Transcendental Idealism

EMERSON thought that human beings, as thinkers, naturally divided into two sects, Materialists and Idealists, and that the chief mark of a Transcendentalist was his idealism. "He does not deny sensuous fact: by no means," said Emerson, "but he will not see that alone." For the American Transcendentalist the universe was in its deepest reaches spiritual in nature. "His experience," Emerson went on to say,

> inclines him to behold the procession of facts you call the world, as flowing perpetually outward from an invisible, unsounded centre in himself, centre alike of him and of them, and necessitating him to regard all things as having a subjective or relative existence, relative to that aforesaid Unknown Centre of him.

To show how seriously Emerson took his idealism, Oliver Wendell Holmes, no devotee of the Newness himself, once told a whimsical story about how Emerson transcendentalized while taking an excursion in the

woods with some youngsters. "Boys," said Emerson,
after bidding them take off their hats as they entered the
woods,

> here we recognize the presence of the Universal
> Spirit. The breeze says to us in its own language,
> How d'ye do? How d'ye do? and we have already
> taken our hats off and are answering it with our own
> How d'ye do? How d'ye do? And all the waving
> branches of the trees, and all the flowers, and the
> field of corn yonder, and the singing brook, and the
> insect and the bird,—every living thing and things
> we call inanimate feel the same divine universal im-
> pulse while they join with us, and we with them, in
> the greeting which is the salutation of the Universal
> Spirit.

It is difficult, to be sure, to visualize Emerson, with his
Yankee reserve, in such a jaunty mood; still, the point of
Holmes's story is valid enough. Emerson—and his fellow
Transcendentalists—did believe deeply in the world as
spirit. For them, the Understanding saw only the material world with its solid objects and events, but Reason
fathomed the spiritual reality underneath. And from
Reason's basic perception that mind was "the only reality,
of which men and all other natures are better or worse
reflectors," flowed everything else in the Transcendentalist outlook. The Transcendentalists had an epistemology in Reason and Understanding; in Universal Spirit
they had a metaphysics.

Metaphysicians, however, the Transcendentalists emphatically were not; not even Emerson. In his *Transcendentalism in New England* (1876), Octavius Brooks
Frothingham, one of the second generation of Transcendentalists, attempted to classify the leading exponents of the New Views: Alcott as Mystic, Fuller as Critic,

Parker as Preacher, Ripley as Man of Letters, and Emerson, heading the list, as Seer. Frothingham was wise to call Emerson a seer rather than a philosopher. Though unquestionably the most gifted thinker of the group, Emerson was admittedly no philosopher like his masters Plato and Kant. Even as a young man he recognized that his was not the cast of mind which produced philosophical treatises. "Who has not looked into a metaphysical book?" he once asked. "And what sensible man ever looked twice?" Emerson did, in fact, look twice, even thrice, into metaphysical books, but like all the Transcendentalists he preferred moral imagination to discursive reasoning and poetry to philosophy. He had a feeling that technical metaphysics was cold, surgical, and remote from life and that metaphysicians professed a completeness and certainty of knowledge which was unwarranted. They were like "gnats grasping the world." The wide, wide world resisted systematizing. "I am a fragment," said Emerson of his own pronouncements, "and this is a fragment of me." The Understanding simply could not answer the big questions about life. "No power of genius has ever yet had the smallest success in explaining existence. The perfect enigma remains." For the Understanding, at any rate, the world was and always would be a riddle. For Reason, however, the sphinx did yield up its mystery: at the heart of things dwelt an ineffable spirit which animated all creation. The Transcendentalists differed among themselves about many things but on one point they were in fundamental agreement: there was a divine energy immanent in nature and in man, giving them meaning, purpose, and direction. For the Transcendentalists (and nineteenth-century Romantics generally) the organic metaphor replaced the mechanical. In place of the clockwork universe of the eighteenth-century Enlightenment they put a universe that was living, growing, and endlessly advancing from lower to higher forms. Transcendentalism rested on an exalted view of creation. It is a view which scarcely survives today in the Western world, partly because man has interposed so much of his own perishable handiwork between himself and the natural world.

Universal Spirit

To show how multifarious the divine creative energy shaping the universe was, the Transcendentalists referred to it in innumerable ways: as Supreme Being, Over-Soul, Creator, Original Cause, Universal Power, Highest Law, Supreme Mind, Eternal Reason, Universal Consciousness, Universal Spirit, and God. It was the cause, creator, essence, animator, shaper, and sustainer of all things. It dwelt in the highest laws and in the lowliest particles. From it flowed all truth, beauty, and goodness. Alcott strove hard to explicate it:

> ... that power which pulsates in all life, animates and builds all organizations, shall manifest itself as one universal deific energy, present alike at the outskirts and centre of the universe, whose centre and circumference are one; omniscient, omnipotent, self-subsisting, uncontained, yet containing all things in the unbroken synthesis of its being.

The belief that the natural world was a projection and symbol of Universal Spirit was the most obvious sign of being a Transcendentalist. Each Transcendentalist had his own way of putting it. Parker put it plainly and simply: "The fullness of the divine energy flows inexhaustibly into the crystal of the rock, the juices of the plant, the splendor of the stars, the life of the Bee and Behemoth." His colleagues expressed it more poetically. Nature for Emerson was the externalization of the soul, mind precipitated, the incarnation of a thought, the plantations of God. Nature "suggests the absolute," he wrote. "It is a perpetual effect. It is a great shadow pointing always to the sun behind us." In his journal he once queried: "What is there of divine in a load of bricks?" and promptly answered: "Much. All." In *Orphic Sayings*, Alcott, striving hard again to make it all clear, called nature a mystic cipher and hieroglyph of spirit, spirit in magnitude, the Bible of Deity written in things, a revelation of mind, and the flesh of the spirit. "Matter," he said, "is ever pervaded and agitated by the omnipresent soul. All things are instinct with spirit." Christopher Cranch said, "Nature is but a scroll,—God's handwriting thereon"; and Henry Thoreau thought that the "circulations of God" pervaded the physical world. "The earth I trod on," said Thoreau, "is not a dead inert mass. It is a body, has a spirit, is organic. . . ."

It was entirely appropriate that Emerson's first book and the first important Transcendentalist document should be entitled *Nature*. In it, Emerson not only discoursed on the natural world as a source of material abundance, aesthetic pleasure, and scientific truth; he also explored at length—and this was his highest interest—the moral and spiritual meaning inherent in natural phenomena. Words are signs of natural facts, he declared, in a section on "Language"; particular natural facts are the symbols of particular spiritual facts; and nature is the symbol of spirit. He gave numerous illustrations of what he had in mind. Among inanimate objects, a rock represented firmness and a river signified the flux of things. Among living creatures, the fox meant cunning, the snake subtle spite, and the lamb innocence. Our proverbs, each containing a little homily, are drawn from natural events: a rolling stone gathers no moss, make hay while the sun shines, a bird in the hand is worth two in the bush. Even our words for the highest moral conceptions

have a natural origin: the word "right" originally meant
straight, while "wrong" meant crooked; and the word
"spirit" itself meant wind in the beginning. Nature, in
short, was a vast trope. Where Emerson's Puritan
forebears scanned nature for evidences of special provi-
dences, Emerson read it for moral meanings. So did most
of the other Transcendentalists.

Flux, Polarity, Correspondence, and Unity

In addition to exploring nature's symbols, Emerson
liked to investigate what he called the "method of nature." In so doing he inevitably mingled physics and
ethics. Nature's methods, Emerson decided, involved
three basic conceptions: flux, polarity, and correspondence. Of the three, flux had the least ethical import,
though it, too, contained a lesson for mankind. By flux,
Emerson meant the perpetual movement and ceaseless
change found everywhere in the natural world. Nature
was not fixed but fluid; it was like a cataract or a rushing
stream or a field of maize growing in July. Creation was
on wheels, in transit, in rapid metamorphosis, always
passing into something else. Thin or solid, everything
was in flight, casting off old forms, putting on new ones.
The divine circulations never rested or lingered. Every
natural fact was an emanation and that from which it
emanated was an emanation also and from every emanation came a new emanation. One could not, as Heraclitus
noted centuries ago, bathe twice in the same river; a man
could not even see the same object twice. Emerson liked
to remind the sturdy Boston capitalist that no matter how
firmly he laid the foundations of his banking-house or
exchange, both he and his buildings rested on a planet
which went spinning away, "dragging bank and banker
with it at a rate of thousands of miles the hour, he knows
not whither,—a bit of bullet, now glimmering, now

darkling through a small cubic space on the edge of an unimaginable pit of emptiness." Sometimes Emerson used the word "ecstasy" to describe the perpetual whirl of natural events. Nature was ecstatic, he said; it was bursting with creative power. There was an inexhaustible supply of divine energy in the universe and it had a tendency to push its way with irresistible force and utter abandon into every nook and cranny of the natural world, overwhelming everything in its way and transforming everything it encountered. Emerson thought that people would do well to imitate the ecstasy of nature, at least on occasion. If they burst the bounds of the Understanding and permitted Reason to make electric contact with the divine energy pulsating within themselves and linking them with the eternal flux of nature, they, too, might experience ecstasy. (Thoreau described the experience as "a sense of elevation and expansion" which was joyous and all-absorbing, but Parker tended to distrust it as inimical to rational thought.) But at the same time Reason will recognize that the Heraclitean flux is not simply a meaningless flow of pure energy; it will discern the forms and patterns that emerge as the "divine Presence" rushes through the world.

One of the basic patterns was polarity. "The fact of two poles, of two forces, centripetal and centrifugal, is universal," Emerson declared, "and each force by its own activity develops the other." He also referred to the presence of binary opposites everywhere as "undulation"; and when he was not contemplating the flux of things he was looking for "metaphysical antagonists" in nature: action and reaction, darkness and light, heat and cold, the ebb and flow of waters, male and female, the inspiration and expiration of plants and animals, the systole and diastole of the heart, centrifugal and centripetal gravity. "Superimpose magnetism at one end of a needle, the opposite magnetism takes place at the other end," he observed.

> If the south attracts, the north repels. To empty here, you must condense there. An inevitable dualism bisects nature, so that each thing is a half, and suggests another thing to make it whole; as spirit, matter; man, woman; odd, even; subjective, objective; in, out; upper, under; motion, rest; yea, nay.

Emerson believed that polarities appeared in every part and particle of nature as well as in nature as a whole; they were "ingrained in every atom." This meant that every particle was a microcosm containing all the powers and laws of nature within itself. The idea of microcosm was by no means peculiarly Transcendental; it goes back to antiquity. In Greek thought, from Anaximenes to the Stoics and Neoplatonists, and in medieval thought as well, it was common to think of man as a "little world," reflecting or epitomizing in his structure and behavior the macrocosm or "great world." In modern times, however, with the rise of empirical science, the microcosmic view shifted from man to nature; and scientists began to think of every particle of matter as a copy of the whole universe. In the seventeenth century, Johannes Kepler saw the harmony of the spheres reflected in miniature in a snow-crystal and in the nineteenth, French astronomer Pierre Laplace thought scientists some day would be able to demonstrate the "mechanics of the whole universe" from a grain of sand. (Twentieth-century physicists, however, have discovered that the behavior of subatomic particles is at variance with that of heavenly bodies and have abandoned the once-popular analogy between the atom and the solar system.) But the doctrine of microcosm fit in very neatly with the Transcendental sense of the ubiquitousness of divinity and Emerson (who probably learned it from the Greeks) made it a part of his philosophy. God, he said, "reappears with all his parts in every moss and cobweb"; the "whirling bubble on the surface of a brook admits us to the secret of the mechanics of the sky." As he expressed it in his poem, "The Sphinx,"

> Through a thousand voices
>   Spoke the universal dame:
> "Who telleth one of my meanings
>   Is master of all I am."

Emerson, as one would expect, found moral meaning in the concept of polarity on both microcosmic and macrocosmic levels. He linked it with his famous doctrine of compensation which held that there is a balance between good and evil in the world and that perfect justice prevails in the long run. Excess and defect, sweet and sour, wit and folly, good and evil neatly balance each other in human life, according to Emerson, thus reflecting the polarity which is built into the very structure of the natural world.

If Emerson saw a parallel between polarity and compensation, it was because he discerned a correspondence between all physical and moral laws. Science and ethics went hand in hand in the Transcendentalist universe. The correspondence of nature and mind was basic to the Transcendental angle of vision. There was a perpetual league between nature and virtue for the Transcendentalists. The Protean divine energy took the form of physical law in nature and of moral law in man, but the laws were similar in their operation. "The laws of moral nature answer to those of matter as face to face in a glass. . . ," said Emerson.

The axioms of physics translate the laws of ethics. Thus "the whole is greater than its parts"; "reaction is equal to action"; "the smallest weight may be made to lift the greatest, the difference of weight being compensated by time"; and many the like propositions have a much more extensive and universal sense when applied to human life, than when confined to technical use.

The doctrine of correspondence was not new with Emerson. The germs of it could be found in Plato and a theological version of it (which Emerson discarded as too literalistic) appeared in the eighteenth-century Swedish mystic Emanuel Swedenborg. But Emerson, as usual, made the idea peculiarly his own. Collecting specific instances of the correspondence of physical and moral laws became something of a game for him. Gravity, he said, corresponded to truth: both were omnipresent and indestructible and against neither could a blow be struck without its recoiling on the striker. Momentum increased by exact laws in intellectual as well as in mechanical action: every scholar knows that he applies himself coldly and slowly at first to his task, but with the progress of the work his mind becomes heated and it begins to see far and wide as it approaches the completion of the task. Vegetation has its analogue in mental activity: in both you get germination, growth, crossings, blight, and parasites. But mechanical laws also pervade the mind, just as vegetative laws do, for the affinity of thoughts is like the affinity of particles. Moreover, just as the sun hurled out from itself the outer rings of diffuse ether which slowly condensed into planets and moons, so, by a higher force of the same law, the Universal Mind detached numerous minds from itself, and these minds themselves detach thoughts or intellections from themselves, and these thoughts all share something of the power and character of the Universal Mind.

For Transcendentalists like Emerson, then, natural law was essentially ethical in character. Every chemical change, every change of vegetation, and every animal function, said Emerson, "shall hint or thunder to man the laws of right and wrong and echo the Ten Commandments." There was nothing in nature which did not have moral significance for Reason. "The moral law lies at the centre of nature and radiates to the circumference. It is the pith and marrow of every substance, every relation, and every process. All things with which we deal, preach to us. What is a farm but a mute gospel?" Facts were significant for people like Emerson and Thoreau only as they flowered into truths; a natural fact had only half its value until its counterpart, a moral truth, emerged. (As Thoreau freed himself from Emerson's influence, however, he came to resist the tendency to moralize the natural world.) The problem facing the thoroughgoing materialist—explaining how moral values and distinctions between right and wrong can emerge from particles of matter in perpetual motion —was no problem for the Transcendentalist. The primordial atoms themselves, according to Emerson, were prefigured and predetermined to moral issues. Ethics was sovereign in the Transcendental universe.

Emerson undoubtedly overstated the case for correspondence. To assert that the law of gravitation is identical with purity of heart illuminates neither physics nor ethics. To say, moreover, that the Newtonian principle, action equals reaction, is ethical as well as mechanical, is probably false; people do, after all, frequently overreact. The formulations of physicists today, furthermore, are so remote from common-sense notions that they can scarcely be stated in ordinary language, to say nothing of being translated into moral concepts. Nevertheless,

Emerson's marriage of physics and ethics should not be dismissed as mere obscurantism. The quest for unity is perennial among human beings and in speculating about the implications of the science of his day for the humanities Emerson was following a noble tradition in the history of thought. If we assume, as we surely must, that what we (for conceptual purposes) call mind and matter are continuous with each other, there is every reason for thinking, as Emerson did, that the laws governing their respective behavior are closely related. During Emerson's later years, Herbert Spencer, no Transcendentalist, attempted to define evolutionary law in such a way as to subsume both physics and ethics under it; and in the twentieth century John Dewey developed an evolutionary philosophy that emphasized the organic continuity and interaction of "mind" and "matter" at every level of development. By Dewey's day, however, the belief that the laws of nature were eternal and immutable had given way to the view of scientific laws as mathematical formulations of statistical probabilities, and this meant a serious revision in the Emersonian point of view (for which Dewey had considerable respect). Emerson's view of scientific law as fixed and unchanging was, of course, unexceptionable for his day. But his deep-seated feeling for the endless flux of things has a distinctly modern (and Deweyan) tone.

When it came to metaphysics, Emersonian Transcendentalists faced a serious problem which they never entirely solved: Did they idealize and moralize the physical world out of existence? Emerson thought it was possible he had. A "noble doubt" as to whether nature outwardly existed, he said, inevitably occurred to thoughtful people; he agreed with Turgot in thinking that a person who never doubted the existence of matter had no aptitude for metaphysical inquiries. But from one point of view, Emerson considered the question of matter's existence unimportant. So long as we can count on the stability of nature and the permanence of its laws, he said, it really matters not whether nature has a substantial existence without or is only "in the apocalypse of the mind." Still, Emerson was convinced that nature was phenomenal, not substantial, and that it could be known only as it appears to us in our sense impressions. He was Kantian to that extent. (So was Thoreau: "Packed in my mind," he wrote, "lie all the clothes which outward nature wears.") But unlike Kant, he liked to toy with the idea that the phenomenal world was only the projection of the mind of man, and at times his language bordered on subjective idealism. He frequently called attention to the fact that our moods and frame of mind color our perception of reality, and he once wrote that nature, like literature, was a "subjective" phenomenon. We see mediately, not directly, he declared, and we have no means of correcting these "colored and distorted lenses which we are" or of computing the amount of their errors. Perhaps, then, these "subject-lenses" have a creative power and there are no real objects outside of ourselves in the universe. "What if you shall come to realize," he asked, "that the play and playground of all this pompous history are radiations from yourself, and that the sun borrows his beams?" It was foolish for a person to praise or blame events; he should recognize that "he only is real, and the world his mirror and echo." Still, Emerson only occasionally toyed with solipsism this way. Most of the time he acknowledged that nature was separate and distinct from man, that it was in many respects independent of the human will, and that its "serene order is inviolable by us." He never walked absentmindedly into a tree as his friend Elizabeth Peabody did on one occasion. "The existing world is not a dream," he exclaimed, "and cannot with impunity be treated as a dream." The phenomenal world was real enough. "I have no hatred to the round earth and its gray mountains," he declared.

> I see well enough the sand-hill opposite my window. I see with as much pleasure as another a field of corn or a rich pasture, whilst I dispute their absolute being. Their phenomenal being I no more dispute than I do my own. I do not dispute, but point out the just way of viewing them.

The just way was to view nature as the objectification of Universal Spirit, the "projection of God in the unconscious," and the "expositor of the divine mind." The Transcendentalist tendency was toward objective idealism, though Emersonians were not much concerned with philosophical labels.

As objective idealists, the Transcendentalists placed great emphasis on the unity as well as the variety of nature. Nature's method, they thought, included not only flux, polarity, and correspondence; it also involved what Emerson called "*all for each and each for all*." So long as one attended only to the variety of things he was missing the true meaning of nature. "There is a perfect solidarity," declared Emerson. "You cannot detach an atom from its holdings, or strip off from it the electricity, gravitation, chemic affinity or the relation to light and heat and leave the atom bare. No, it brings with it its universal ties." In his poem "Xenophanes," Emerson made the point (a favorite one with him) that all things—bird, beast, and flower, song, picture, form, space, thought, and character—deceive us, seeming to be many things when they actually are but one, and that nature is "an infinite paroquet," which repeats one note through her vast and crowded whole. Everything in nature, he was fond of pointing out, was related to the whole and partook of the perfection of the whole. "Nothing is quite beautiful alone," he said; "nothing but is beautiful in the whole." Failure to recognize this basic unity of things produced a mean, partial, and distorted view of creation. The Transcendentalist, moreover, believed in the essential goodness as well as the fundamental unity of creation. In *Walden*, Thoreau spoke of the "indescribable innocence and beneficence of Nature"; and Emerson affirmed that "there is intelligence and good will at the heart of things." To meliorate, Emerson said, was a law of nature; there was a "great and beneficent and progressive necessity" ever at work in the world, "indicating the way upward from the invisible protoplasm to the highest organism. . . ." Emerson's faith in "beneficent tendency" and "beneficent necessity" was profound, and most Transcendentalists agreed with him in affirming the goodness of things.

Human Divinity, Pantheism, and Mysticism

Transcendental optimism extended to man as well as to nature, for apostles of the Newness believed that the Universal Spirit dwelt within human beings as well as in nature. Men and women, to the Transcendentalists, were fundamentally divine; they were partakers of the Divine Nature and incarnations of the Universal Mind. Emerson thought that the "highest revelation" was that God was in every person. "I am divine," he declared. "Through me God acts; through me, he speaks. Would you see God, see me. . . ." Parker's view was the same. "I think God is immanent in man," he told the Reverend Samuel J. May; "yes, in *men*—most in the greatest, truest, best men." An individual person, said Emerson, consisted of both a momentary arrest or fixation of certain atoms drawn from nature in a particular body and a temporary concentration of certain spiritual powers drawn from the Universal Spirit in a particular soul. His body was part of nature, obeying the laws of matter, and his soul was part of the Over-Soul, governed by the laws of spirit. The individual soul was not an organ, according to Emerson,

> but animates and exercises all the organs; is not a function, like the power of memory, of calculation, or comparison, but uses these as hands and feet; is not a faculty, but a light; is not the intellect or the will, but the master of the intellect or the will; is the background of our being, in which they lie—an immensity not possessed and cannot be possessed. From within or from behind, a light shines through us upon things and makes us aware that we are nothing, but the light is all.

The soul was thus both life spirit (animating all the organs) and spiritual vision (a light shining upon things). As the latter, it was identical with Reason. Through his Reason every individual had access to the Universal Mind. The intuitive insights into spiritual truth achieved by Reason were in the final analysis revelations vouchsafed to man by Universal Mind. There was something of the Quaker Inner Light in the Transcendental concept of inspired Reason. There was also something democratic about it. The democrat, Brownson declared, believes that Reason "shines into the heart of every man, and that truth lights her torch in the inner temple of every man's soul, whether patrician or plebeian, a shepherd or a philosopher, a Croesus or a beggar."

The implications of the Transcendental faith in the divinity of man were momentous. Transcendentalism clearly opened the road to both pantheism and mysticism. It could be said, on Transcendental principles, that if an individual surrendered himself utterly to the divine currents circulating within him, he, in effect, became God. Emerson did not shrink from this conclusion. "I am God in nature," he once wrote; "I am a weed by the wall." On another occasion he exclaimed:

> I behold with awe and delight many illustrations of the One Universal Mind. I see my being imbedded in it; as a plant in the earth so I grow in God. I am only a form of him. He is the soul of me. I can even with a mountainous aspiring say, *I am God*, by transferring my *me* out of the flimsy and unclean precinct of the body. . . .

Does this mean that Transcendentalists like Emerson were pantheists, as Andrews Norton and other Unitarian critics of the New Views charged? Brownson emphatically denied that Transcendentalism was pantheistic. "Pantheism," he said, "considers the universe as God," whereas Transcendentalism "presents God as the cause, and the universe as the effect." God was as inseparable from the universe as a cause was inseparable from its effect, Brownson explained, but it was wrong to identify him with the universe, as the pantheists did.

> The universe . . . is his intention. It is what he will, and he is in it, the substance of his volition; it is what he speaks, and he is in it, as a man is in his words; but he is distinct from it, by all the distinction there is between the energy that wills, and that which is willed, between him who speaks and the words he utters.

Parker regarded himself as a theist, not a pantheist, and regarded Emerson as one, too, though with wayward tendencies. Emerson, when young, had feared that

"Pantheism leads to Atheism," but in his maturity frequently talked like a pantheist. "In the woods, this afternoon," he once wrote, "it seemed plain to me that most men were pantheists at heart, say what they might of their own theism. No other path is, indeed, open for them to the One, intellectually at least." On the other hand, because of occasional vagueness of language, he gave the impression at times that he regarded God as separate from creation and that he even believed in a personal God. But he was not really a theist. Most of the time he emphasized immanence rather than transcendence and his inclinations were toward pantheism. "When I speak of God," he said once, "I prefer to say It—It." And he was fascinated by the possibilities of a mystical union of the individual soul with the Universal Spirit pervading creation.

The mystical consciousness, a nonempirical and nonrational mode of apprehending reality, was bound to interest Transcendentalists who were eager to pierce to the heart of things by means of intuitive Reason. The central aim of the mystical experience—an immediate grasp of the undifferentiated unity of the universe as a whole—was also appealing to Transcendentalists like Emerson and Alcott, who had strong leanings toward monism. Mysticism has tended to fall generally into two categories, extrovertive and introvertive, and the Transcendentalists were interested in both. The former, in which the mystic looks outward through his physical senses and discerns the overarching unity pervading the variety of things, is a lower form of mystical consciousness because it includes ordinary sense perception. In introvertive mysticism, the higher form, the mystic eliminates all sensations, feelings, and thoughts and, turning inward, discovers the One, the basic unity, in the depths of himself and merges his individuality with it. The mystic finds it almost impossible to describe his experience properly; he calls it ineffable. To the non-mystic, of course, the mystic's experience may seem to be simply a subjective state of mind without any validity whatsoever as a report on the ultimate nature of things. As William James observed, the experience may be authoritative for the mystic, but it cannot be regarded as having any authority for the nonmystic. Still, the quest for unity has been fundamental in religion, philosophy, and science in all cultures, and the American Transcendentalist believed that the mystical road toward the One deserved serious consideration just as the empirical and the conceptual roads did.

Some of the Transcendentalists (Emerson, Alcott, and Thoreau, in particular) read deeply in the mystical literature of the past and took a special interest in such great mystics as Plotinus, Swedenborg, and Jakob Böhme. Some of them also recorded experiences of their own from time to time or wrote poems which contained distinctly mystical overtones, especially of the extrovertive type. On at least one occasion Margaret Fuller had an experience resembling the introvertive "union" of the Neoplatonists with the Divine One ("I was for that hour taken up into God," she reported), which she felt made a crucial change in her life. Parker also at times expressed himself in thoroughly mystical language ("Man is at one with God, and He is All in All"), though O. B. Frothingham was undoubtedly right in regarding him as "the opposite of a mystic" because of his predilection for empirical facts and his distrust of "ecstasy." Once, in an argument with Alcott, who thought of himself as a mystic, Parker "wound himself around Alcott like an anaconda," Emerson reported; "you could hear poor Alcott's bones crunch." Frothingham called Alcott the mystic of the group, but he did not bring much evidence to support his characterization. Still, Alcott was well-read in the ancient and modern mystics, was sympathetic to the mystical experience, and on one or two occasions experienced periods of illumination ("introversion" was his word for it), in which it was "no longer Many but One with us," and he perceived the universe as one vast spinal column. (After one such introversion his wife promptly sent him packing for a visit to Emerson.) At the Concord School of Philosophy, which Alcott helped found after the Civil War, two speakers once got into a heated argument, and when Alcott, the chairman, suggested a way of harmonizing their views, they said they didn't understand what he meant. "Well, I don't know as I know what I mean myself," Alcott said ruefully, and, as the audience tittered, he explained: "I am a 'mystic,' you know." But Alcott's mysticism was mild indeed compared to that of Jones Very, who often sat long hours alone in his room, quiet and passive, trying to suspend his will and become the mere instrument of Universal Spirit. Emerson liked some of Very's writings and decided that "monomania or mono *Sania* he is a very remarkable person," and helped him publish a book of poetry and essays. But when Very announced that he was a "newborn bard of the Holy Ghost" and proclaimed his identification with Christ, he lost his job teaching Greek at Harvard and was forced to spend a month in Charleston's McLean Hospital.

Emerson and Thoreau had as deep an interest in mysticism as Alcott, though with them, as with most of the Transcendentalists, mysticism was only a minor strain in their lives. Thoreau called himself "a mystic, a transcendentalist, and a natural philosopher to boot," and said that "rude and careless as I am, I would fain practice the *Yoga* faithfully." To some extent Thoreau did practice *Yoga* (which aims, through physical and spiritual exercises, to attain union with Brahman) at Walden. He dieted, meditated, went down to the pond every day, like a Hindu in Benares, for morning ablutions ("a religious exercise, one of the best things which I did"), and on at least one occasion sat in his sunny doorway by the pond for a whole morning utterly unconscious of the passage of time. In his journal for 1856, he also reported that he had been "expanded and infinitely and divinely related for a brief season." The Hindu scriptures were among his favorite reading. Emerson also responded warmly to Hindu religious writings, and he was interested enough in Swedenborg, the eighteenth-century Swedish scientist, inventor, and mystic, to devote a whole chapter to him in *Representative Men* (1850). But Emerson was not entirely favorable to Swedenborg. He acknowledged the "unquestionable increase of mental power" resulting from Swedenborg's religious illuminations, but he also saw something morbid and pathological about them. He was similarly ambivalent about Jakob Böhme, seventeenth-century German mystic, whom he otherwise admired, because of his "narrowness and incommunicableness" and his tendency to "egotism and insanity." And when it came to the popular "occult," Emerson was downright derisive, for he thought it trivialized the universe, and he called it "the Rat-revelation, the gospel that comes by taps in the wall, and thumps in the table-drawer." (Fuller and Alcott were more sympathetic to it, and Parker urged a scientific study of it.)

Did Emerson, like Margaret Fuller, Alcott, and Thoreau, ever have any personal experiences of his own that might be called "mystical"? Here and there one encounters in Emerson's essays passages with mystical overtones that sound autobiographical; but they may have expressed a romantic exhilaration with natural beauty rather than a mystic state of mind. Perhaps the most famous such passage appears in *Nature*:

> Standing on the bare ground,—my head bathed by the blithe air, and uplifted into infinite space,—all mean egotism vanishes. I become a transparent

eye-ball. I am nothing; I see all; the currents of the Universal Being circulate through me; I am part or parcel of God.

But the "eyeball" metaphor Emerson borrowed from Plotinus and the experience he described was therefore secondhand. Christopher Cranch caricatured the passage in a drawing of a lonely Transcendentalist, consisting mainly of one huge, melancholy eyeball perched on two spindly legs and wearing a hat, but Emerson was as amused by the sketch as anyone else. Emerson was without question deeply religious in his own fashion; but he was a mystic only in the broadest sense of the word. Though he once reported in his journal that "a certain wandering light comes to me which I instantly perceive to be the cause of causes," this kind of experience appears to have been infrequent. The single-minded concentration and severe discipline of the mystic and the subordination of family, friends, community, country, even life itself, to the quest for mystic union with the eternal One formed no part of Emerson's regimen, though he was sympathetic to mystical aspirations. Emerson was more a humanist than a mystic, and so were all the Transcendentalists. "I love life," he once explained to Margaret Fuller; and in his journal he wrote: "Transcendentalism says, the Man is all." William B. Greene came close to the mark when he observed in the *American Whig Review* that, "Pantheism sinks man and nature in God; Materialism sinks God and man in the universe; Transcendentalism sinks God and nature in man." Religion—the teleological view of creation—was basic in Transcendentalism. But it was a foundation for the exaltation of human nature and not an end in itself.

Individuality, Creativity, and Self-Reliance

The Transcendental faith in the divinity of man took both a universalistic and an individualistic form. It was universalistic in that the Universal Spirit which the Transcendentalists believed dwelt within the individual also permeated the physical world and dwelt within other human beings and thus linked the individual to both his natural and his social environments by the closest of ties. (One of the favorite themes of Emerson's poetry was how the individual loses meaning when isolated from relationships with the larger world.) But the Transcendental faith was individualistic as well as universalistic, because it held that each person was a unique manifestation of Universal Spirit at a particular time and place in the world and that his life and work, while forming part of the ongoing processes of the universe, took a form and possessed a quality not found in any other human being. "The divine energy never rests or repeats itself," said Emerson, "but casts its old garb, and reappears, another creature; the old energy in a new form, with all the vigor of the earth; the Ancient of Days in the dew of the morning." Individuality and universality: Transcendentalism maintained a constant tension between the two; it was Emersonian polarity at the highest level. The Transcendentalists were not rugged individualists who sacrificed all social responsibilities for the aggrandizement of the individual; neither did they dissolve the individual in the maternal embrace of the Over-Soul. "But there remains the indefeasible persistency of the individual to be himself," said Emerson. "One leaf, one blade of grass, one meridian, does not resemble another. Every mind is different; and the more it is unfolded, the more pronounced the difference." The Transcendentalists were eager to see youthful minds unfold fruitfully; they thought all men and women had divine possibilities. Each person, Emerson said, was "a new method and distributes things anew"; each person possessed some "triumphant superiority," some "new bias" of faculty, some "new power in nature," had some special aptitude for knowing or doing something in the world. There were vast stores of power and vitality in each man and woman waiting to be developed. Each person contained within himself tremendous potentialities for creative development and self-realization. In the Transcendental philosophy all men were created equal, that is to say, all of them contained the possibility of doing something special and unique with their lives if they but tapped the divine energy within them. (When Rufus Choate spoke of the "glittering generalities" of the Declaration of Independence, Emerson exclaimed: "Glittering generalities!—*rather* blazing UBIQUITIES!"

How did one avail oneself of this creative energy? By harkening to the still, small voice of Reason within and following its promptings faithfully. Reason (or intuition or instinct) was the key to creativity. The Universal Spirit gave leadings to the individual through his Reason, and Reason was thus the fountainhead of originality. "We lie in the lap of immense intelligence," Emerson declared, "which makes us receivers of its truth and organs of its activity." Every person had access to Universal Spirit, but he had to transcend his Understanding, which bound him too closely to custom, tradition, and the received wisdom of the day, if he was to permit his Reason to become a channel for the currents of Universal Spirit moving within him. "I have been forced to appeal from tradition and authority to the Universal Reason," cried Brownson, "a ray of which shines into the heart of every man that cometh into the world. . . ." One should never "dismiss, with haste, the visions which flash and sparkle" across one's sky, Emerson advised; "but observe them, approach them, domesticate them, brood on them, and draw out of the past, genuine life for the present hour." The Transcendentalists thought that Universal Spirit expressing itself through human Reason was the source of imaginative insight into spiritual truth and the inspiration for all great art, science, and literature. Man's Reason, said Emerson, was "a spark at which all the illuminations of human arts and sciences were kindled." The Transcendentalist, he explained, "believes in miracles, in the perpetual openness of the human mind to new influx of light and power; he believes in inspiration and ecstasy." God, according to Parker, "inspires men, makes revelation of truth," but this revelation took various forms and was modified by the country, character, education, and individual peculiarities of the person receiving it. Universal Spirit had a fondness for variety of expression. And this meant that each individual had a call to do something unique in the world. "Each man has his own vocation," said Emerson. "The talent is the call." The Transcendentalists advised young people to discover what their own special talents and aptitudes were and then to concentrate on developing them to the utmost. They transcendentalized the old Puritan doctrine of calling by identifying glorification of God with creative expression of the individual. "Each man has an aptitude born with him," said Emerson confidently. "Do your work." In his essay "Self-Reliance," he put it a little differently: "But do your thing, and I shall know you. . . ."

Doing one's thing was no easy task; it meant being resolutely independent and self-reliant in both thought and action. It meant basing one's thoughts and deeds on resources growing naturally out of the depths of one's own personality and not drawn from one's peer group. "Engage in nothing that cripples or degrades you," advised Alcott. "Your first duty is self-culture, self-exaltation: you may not violate this high trust." Thoreau urged people to "keep strictly onward in that path alone which your genius points out. Do the things that lie nearest to you, but which are difficult to do." To believe "your own thought," said Emerson, "to believe that what is true for you in your private heart is true for all men —that is genius." Borrowing one's opinions from other people and acting merely in response to outside pressures not only falsified one's true being; it also squandered vital personal energy and prevented an individual from making his own unique contribution to the world. "It is simpler to be self-dependent," Emerson contended.

> The height, the deity of man is to be self-sustained, to need no gifts, no foreign force. Society is good when it does not violate me, but best when it is likest to solitude; let the soul be erect, and all things will go well. You think me the child of my circumstances; I make my circumstances.

Emerson was exaggerating here the power of the individual to control his circumstances, just as in other contexts he exaggerated the submergence of the individual in the "all-absorbing Unity" of the world. But he felt strongly that the point should be made emphatically: each person is in some sense different from every other person, and he should accept his individuality as an opportunity, not a handicap, learn to "detect and watch that gleam of light which flashes across his mind from within," and develop the courage and strength to live by his own deepest insights even if they run counter to the views of family, friends, and community.

In "Self-Reliance," perhaps his most famous essay, Emerson explored at length the ramifications of an ethic of self-trust. Self-reliance, he said, required one to "take himself for better or worse as his portion." It meant being a nonconformist if the integrity of one's mind was at stake. It demanded that one keep serenely independent in the midst of the crowd, resist the pressure of "communities of opinion," and refuse to wear the "prison-uniform" of parties. It meant refusing to observe customs that have become dead for you. It required one to speak at all times "in hard words" what he honestly believes, without caring whether he was misunderstood and without straining for a "foolish consistency" in his utterances. It meant refusing to be intimidated by the printed word. It entailed putting the truth above amicable relations with other people and refusing to put on the "foolish face of praise" or to affect hospitality and good will where these are not sincerely felt. It involved rejection of popular standards whenever they clash with principles. It demanded, in short, as Emerson acknowledged, "something godlike in him who has cast off the common motives of humanity and has ventured to trust himself for a taskmaster." But he promised that with the exercise of self-trust, new powers would appear and that it would work a revolution in religion, education, artistic endeavor, modes of living, and social relations.

But if every person follows his own instincts regardless of his fellows, what happens to the community? And what guarantee is there that an individual's deepest motivations are trustworthy? Emerson admitted that the self-reliant Transcendentalist was open to the charge of antinomianism but he refused to retreat from his position. The only right, he affirmed, was "what is after my constitution," and the only wrong was "what is against it." A person must "carry himself in the presence of all opposition as if every thing were titular and ephemeral but he." He was even to shun father, mother, wife, and brother when his genius called him, said Emerson, and write "whim" on the doorpost if people, not comprehending, demanded explanations. If it was suggested that the impulses he was relying on came from below, not from above, then the Transcendentalist could only say, "They do not seem to me to be such; but if I am the Devil's child, I will live then from the Devil." He was not even to be intimidated by the possibility that the "bold sensualist" might "gild his crimes" by rationalizing his behavior in the name of Transcendental self-reliance. But, in point of fact, Emerson did not have the slightest fear that the kind of self-reliance he was advocating promoted moral anarchism. Self-reliance, to the Transcendentalists, meant reliance on intuition, which in turn meant reliance on the promptings of the Universal Spirit within the individual. Self-trust was, in effect, God-trust, and it led one into the realm of universal moral principles. The Universal Spirit, though individuating itself in particular persons, had the same message for everyone as it moved ever onward and upward. "There is one spirit through myriad mouths . . . ," wrote Emerson. "Every word of truth that is spoken by man's lips is from God. Every thought that is true is from God. Every right act is from God. . . . There is but one source of power, that is God." In obeying the spirit within, then, the individual was choosing the rocky road of the categorical imperative. As to why Universal Spirit inspired some individuals and not others, Emerson had no answer. Inspiration, he decided, was "coy and capricious," and its "arts and methods of working" remained a mystery. "There is the incoming or receding of God; that is all we can affirm; and we can show neither how nor why." Every person, Emerson said, made a distinction between the voluntary acts of his mind (Understanding) and his involuntary perceptions (Reason), and it was to the latter that "a perfect faith is due." Why do some people trust their intuitions and others brush them aside? Again Emerson pleaded ignorance:

If you say, "The acceptance of the vision is also the act of God:" I shall not seek to penetrate the mystery, I admit the force of what you say. If you ask, "How can any rules be given for the attainment of gifts so sublime?" I shall only remark that the solicitations of this spirit, so long as there is life, are never forborne. Tenderly, tenderly, they woo and court us from every object in nature, from every fact in life, from every thought in the mind. The one condition coupled with the gift of truth is its use. . . .

The Transcendental Ethic and Aesthetic

Using the gift of truth was enormously difficult; the Transcendentalists never pretended otherwise. Self-reliance was a tough taskmaster. For all the appeals to instinct, feeling, intuition, and natural self-expression in Transcendentalism, there was a distinct note of austerity in the movement. Though accused by critics (both then and now) of viewing life through rose-colored glasses, the Transcendentalists never said that it was easy to live by their principles. In many respects Transcendentalism was closer to Stoicism in its ethical counsels than to any other philosophy. It demanded courage, strength, honor, equanimity, integrity, magnanimity, and adherence to high principle at all times and in all areas of life. "What is *moral*?" asked Emerson. "It is the respecting in action catholic or universal ends. Hear the definition which Kant gives of moral conduct: 'Act always so that the immediate motive of thy will may become a universal rule for all intelligent beings.'" And he went on to explain:

All the virtues are special directions of this motive; justice is the application of this good of the whole to the affairs of each one; courage is contempt of danger in the determination to see this good of the whole enacted; love is delight in the preference of that benefit redounding to another over the securing of our own share; humility is a sentiment of our insignificance when the benefit of the universe is considered.

It is clear that when writers like Emerson and Thoreau transcendentalized, they frequently made incredibly high demands on human nature and called for a level of intellection and behavior that was impossible (and probably undesirable) to sustain for any length of time. Take, for example, their view of friendship. In his essay "Friendship," for *Essays, First Series* (1841), Emerson conceded that tenderness, as well as truth, was indispensable among friends, but his main stress was on the austerity of the relationship. All association was a compromise, he warned, and as people approached each other their character tended to deteriorate. "The condition which high friendship demands," he said, "is ability to do without it." Emerson did not think that "rash personal relations" were essential to friendship; a simple exchange of letters was more "spiritual" than direct contact and better calculated to keep the relationship "poetic, pure, universal and great as nature itself." It was wise, moreover, to break off relations if one was becoming too dependent on a friend. The upshot:

I do then with my friends as I do with my books. I would have them where I can find them, but I seldom use them. We must have society on our own terms and admit or exclude it on the slightest cause. I cannot afford to speak much with my friend. If he is great he makes me so great that I cannot descend to converse.

* * *

Margaret Fuller adored Emerson, but she feared that he had "raised himself too early to the perpendicular and did not lie along the ground long enough to hear the secret whispers of our parent life." (Once, when she was a house guest of the Emersons, she and Emerson communicated with each other by letters, with young Waldo serving as mail boy.) Thoreau's view of friendship was equally perpendicular. In a long passage on the subject in *A Week on the Concord and Merrimack Rivers*, Thoreau followed Emerson in placing friendship on such a high level of ideality that intimate relations were almost by definition ruled out. Kindness, Thoreau declared, formed no part of friendship; indeed, a favor from a friend, he said, would destroy the relationship. The Transcendental view of friendship (at least in the abstract) so outraged Herman Melville that he included a long satire on it in *The Confidence Man* (1857), in which he made the point that if you were a Transcendentalist you were obliged to turn to strangers rather than to your "celestial friends" when in trouble.

Emerson admitted frankly that there was an antisocial side to Transcendentalism. The Transcendentalist, he said, was neither good citizen nor good member of society, and he didn't even like to vote. It was impossible for him to take seriously most "causes" that people proposed for his consideration; he would not "quit his belief that a popgun is a popgun, though the ancient and honorable of the earth affirm it to be the crack of doom." For the Transcendentalists, the gifts of life seemed

> too rich to be squandered on such trifles as you propose to them. What you call your fundamental institutions, your great and holy causes, seem to them great abuses, and, when nearly seen, paltry matters. Each "cause," as it is called,—say Abolition,

Temperance, say Calvinism, or Unitarianism,—becomes speedily a little shop, where the article, let it have been at first never so subtle and ethereal, is now made up into portable and convenient cakes, and retailed in small quantities to suit purchasers. You make very free use of these words "great" and "holy", but few things appear to them such. Few persons have any magnificence of nature to inspire enthusiasm, and the philanthropies and charities have a certain air of quackery.

Emerson did not deny that his attitude smacked of social irresponsibility, but he said stoutly: "Be it so: I can sit in a corner and *perish* (as you call it), but I will not move until I have the highest command."

When the Transcendentalists judged American life by the highest command, they found it woefully lacking in quality. It was too materialistic, for one thing. The passion for "*le make-money*," as a French traveler called it, was inordinate, public and private avarice were rampant, and utilitarian values dominant everywhere. A "vulgar prosperity," Emerson feared, was retrograding to barbarism in Jacksonian America. The American people, for another thing, were seriously deficient in self-respect. The American freeman, said Emerson, was "timid, imitative, tame," and he looked to Europe, especially England, for all his ideas and culture. The Transcendentalists, as men and women of letters, were especially vexed by the derivative nature of most American art and literature in the first part of the nineteenth century, and they were anxious to encourage (and practice personally) self-reliance in artistic endeavor as in other areas of life. The Transcendental aesthetic centered around the idea of organic growth. The inspiration for genuine art, the Transcendentalists held, came from within the depths of one's being and took exterior form freely and naturally so long as the artist faithfully followed the beckonings of the creative spirit within, which was attempting to express itself, through him, in the idiom of his particular time and place. "It is not metres, but a metre-making argument that makes a poem," declared Emerson, "—a thought so passionate and alive that like the spirit of a plant or an animal, it has an architecture of its own, and adorns nature with a new thing." But most American art was borrowed, not inspired; it was dull and provincial, Thoreau thought, partly because Americans were too narrowly devoted to economic enterprise and partly because they did not find their standards at home. The Transcendentalists called for Newness in art and literature as well as in religion and philosophy. Emerson thought that Americans had listened too long to "the courtly muses of Europe," Brownson held that England's aristocratic culture "cramps our national genius" and "exercises a tyrannical sway over the American mind," and Margaret Fuller pointed out that only "fresh currents of life" in America itself could produce a fresh and vital American culture. Margaret Fuller, the best Transcendental literary critic, was harsh in her judgment of popular American poets of her day. James Russell Lowell possessed "facility at versification," she wrote, but not much else; his poetry was "stereotyped; his thought sounds no depth; and posterity will not remember him." As for Henry Wadsworth Longfellow, he, too, was artificial and imitative: "He has no style of his own, growing out of his own experience and observation of nature. Nature with him, whether human or external, is always seen through the windows of literature."

Emerson was not so outspoken as Margaret Fuller, but he shared her concern for the development of an authentic American culture. His Phi Beta Kappa address

"The American Scholar" (1837) was in part a plea for originality in American letters. Oliver Wendell Holmes called it an "intellectual declaration of American independence." Since the Transcendentalists thought of all the world and everything in it as a miracle, it is not surprising that Emerson proposed that American artists begin exploring "the near, the low, the common" as sources for their work, for, as he said, things near were "not less beautiful and wondrous" than things remote. "What would we really know the meaning of?" he exclaimed. "The meal in the firkin; the milk in the pan; the ballad in the street; the news of the boat; the glance of the eye; the form and gait of the body. . . ." Even the factory village and the railway could become part of great poetry. In "The Poet" (1844), Emerson called for a poet who would dare to take the carnival of American life, with all its barbarism and materialism, as his subject and probe to the great beating heart beneath the surface:

Banks and tariffs, the newspaper and caucus, Methodism and Unitarianism, are flat and dull to dull people, but rest on the same foundations of wonder as the town of Troy and the temple of Delphi, and are as swiftly passing away. Our log-rolling, our stumps and their politics, our fisheries, our Negroes and Indians, our boats and our repudiations, the wrath of rogues and the pusillanimity of honest men, the northern trade, the southern planting, the western clearing, Oregon and Texas, are yet unsung. Yet America is a poem in our eyes; its ample geography dazzles the imagination, and it will not wait long for meters.

But it was not only in art and literature that the Transcendentalists called for a fresh spirit and new themes. They also put forth New Views about society and politics and though their primary interests were religious and literary they found themselves inevitably involved in the agitation for humanitarian reform during the Age of Jackson. "The mind now thinks, now acts," Emerson reminded students in his Phi Beta Kappa address; "and each fit reproduces the other. Thinking is a function. Living is functionary. A great soul will be strong to live as well as strong to think." The Transcendental conscience was social as well as individual; the Transcendental mind was practical as well as idealistic.

CHAPTER FOUR

Social Reform

"IN the history of the world the doctrine of Reform had never such scope as at the present hour," Emerson wrote in *The Dial* for April, 1841. It seemed to him as if customs, traditions, and institutions everywhere "hear the trumpet and must rush to judgment, —Christianity, the laws, commerce, schools, the farm, the laboratory; and not a kingdom, town, statute, rite, calling, man, or woman, but is threatened by the new spirit." The Transcendentalists were not the only people offering the nation New Views during the Age of Jackson. Not only were Jacksonian Democrats carrying on the struggle against corporate privilege and money power; a series of piecemeal reforms—women's rights, temperance, prison reform, abolitionism, children's aid, and educational reform—was also agitating the nation. At the same time, some people, distressed by the acquisitive spirit and repelled by industrialism, retreated to communities of their own devising to experiment in utopian living. The Transcendentalists were deeply affected by the meliorative mood pervading Jacksonian America, and nearly all of them accepted the "Sisterhood of Reforms" of their day. Some of them also participated in projects for community-building. "We are all a little wild here with numberless projects of social reform," Emerson wrote Carlyle. "Not a reading man but has a draft of a new community in his waistcoat pocket." He was amused by the people he saw at a big reform rally in Boston—"Madmen, madwomen, men with beards, Dunkers, Muggletonians, Come-outers, Groaners, Agrarians, Seventh-Day Baptists, Quakers, Abolitionists, Calvinists, Unitarians and Philosophers"—but he was also vastly interested.

Emerson thought there were always two parties in society: "the party of the Past and the party of the Future; the Establishment and the Movement." He also called them the parties of Memory and Hope and the parties of Understanding and Reason. The Transcendentalists regarded themselves as part of the Movement. With reform, however, as with everything else, there was wide divergence of opinion among champions of the Newness. When it came to social action, the Transcendentalists ranged all the way from the severe aloofness of Thoreau (until abolitionism fired his passions) and the sympathetic but detached views of Emerson to the energetic activism of Parker and the communitarian experimentalism of Ripley. As a whole, though, the Transcendentalists were scarcely in good repute with Respectability when it came to social issues. "The view taken of Transcendentalism in State Street," Emerson noted wryly, "is that it threatens to invalidate contracts." But Emerson reciprocated the business community's distrust. "Boston or Brattle Street Christianity," he remarked, "is a compound of force, or the best diagonal line that can be drawn between Jesus Christ and Abbott Lawrence." (A Massachusetts textile magnate of the time.)

Emerson and Reform

For all his amused disdain for the popular wisdom of his day (and especially for that represented by the Unitarian patricians running things in eastern Massachusetts), Emerson faced a serious dilemma when it came to social action. Transcendentalism, as he expounded it in lecture after lecture, was at heart an appeal for moral reform of the individual. There was little or no hope for social betterment, from Emerson's point of view, unless the people making up the social order learned to take their cues from the "great inward Commander" and tried to live by Kantian imperatives. (He would have been appalled by the notion, made popular in the twentieth century, that people should take their cues from a great outward commander.) If members of the Establishment did not obey the highest command, neither, in Emerson's opinion, did participants in the Movement. Emerson frequently found himself berating reformers, even when he sympathized with their aims, for departing from the high principles which he regarded as indispensable for any serious social advance. "The Reformers," he complained,

affirm the inward life, but they do not trust it, but use outward and vulgar means. They do not rely on precisely that strength which wins me to their cause; not on love, not on a principle, but on men, on multitudes, on circumstances, on money, on party; that is, on fear, on wrath, and pride. . . .

He concluded that most reformers were narrow-minded, self-pleasing, and arrogant and that the circumstantial freedom for which they were struggling was trivial compared to the inner freedom one attains by transcending mere circumstances and living by high principle.

Motives are always mixed; and Emerson was shrewd in detecting the self-serving elements creeping inevitably into the motivations of even the most idealistic of reformers. Still, were there not self-regarding motives in Emerson's own bent for detachment? At the very least, did not abstention from active reform free him to do what he really enjoyed doing most—reading great works of literature, keeping a journal, writing poems, and composing moral lectures and essays? Emerson would not have denied this; in fact, he freely admitted his predilection for the study over the streets. He was, in short, primarily a man of letters, not a social activist. Being a poet was his true vocation ("I am not a great poet," he told Elizabeth Peabody, "but whatever is of me is a poet"), and it would be violating his deepest instincts to depart from that sacred calling. Emerson begged his friends in reform to understand his position. He did not question the necessity for a Transcendentalist like himself to "succor the helpless and oppressed; always to throw himself on the side of weakness, of youth, of hope; on the liberal, on the expansive side, never on the defensive, the conserving, the timorous, the lock-and-bolt system." But like everyone else, including reformers, he must also remain true to his inward light and save his vital energy for his proper work. "More than our goodwill," he explained, "we may not be able to give. We have our own affairs, our own genius, which chains each to his proper work. We cannot give our life to the cause of the debtor, of the slave, or the pauper as another is doing. . . ." Artistic endeavor was just as important to civilized living as reform. Still, he promised "not to blaspheme the sentiment and the work" of reformers and "not to throw stumbling-blocks in the way of the abolitionist, the philanthropist; as the organs of influence and opinion are swift to do."

There were more than Transcendental reasons for Emerson's reluctance to get actively involved in reform. Emerson was reared in the staid atmosphere of Boston and Harvard Unitarianism, and he imbibed a social conservatism in his early years that he was never quite able to throw off even after leaving the church. The Unitarian consensus Emerson knew as a young man was elitist in outlook; it stressed leadership by educated people allied with well-to-do merchants, reverence for established institutions, limited individual rights, the sanctity of private property, and the duty of philanthropic stewardship on the part of rich people. James Walker, a Unitarian minister with some friendliness for Transcendentalism, called himself a "good republican," but he emphatically rejected the idea that the noble phrase, "All men are created equal," should ever become the social reality, "All men *die* equal." Yet Transcendentalism, by holding that all men and women had a spark of divinity in them, was both democratic and equalitarian in its basic orientation, and Emerson was well aware of that fact. (He once tried to get his household help to take meals at the family table but the cook adamantly refused to do so.) Still, he tended all of his life to distrust the masses, and he thought the average person was imperceptive, vulgar, and mediocre. "All men think," he said; "but rarely. All men can." Everyone possessed Reason and, through it, equal access to Universal Mind; but the variations in the power of Understanding among people were enormous.

One could not ignore, Emerson warned, the "terrible aristocracy that is in Nature." Emerson had unbounded admiration for individual achievement on a large scale, and he tended to think that a social institution was mainly the "lengthened shadow of one man." He never ceased proclaiming that all men and women had infinite possibilities of development, if they but looked to their inner resources; but he seems to have doubted whether most of them would ever do this, and he took for granted a certain amount of social stratification growing out of differences in individual performance. "Spoons and skimmers may well enough lie together," he said; "but vases and statues must have each its own pedestal."

When it came to politics (the word, he noted, originally meant cunning), he found neither the Democrats nor the Whigs of his day particularly to his liking. The Jacksonian Democrats were crude, rowdy, and unprincipled, he thought, and the Whigs, while having more cultivated leadership, were timorous, negative, merely defensive of property, and obsessed by wealth. Neither party seemed to realize that the state existed not to advance the fortunes of a particular class of people (though Emerson was keenly aware of the economic basis of political parties) but to further the development of morally elevated men and women. How the state was to do this Emerson never made quite clear; apparently by leaving people strictly alone. Emerson was strongly laissez-faire in his economic views, and he occasionally had good words to say for the Democratic Party because it supported free trade and the removal of barriers to political and economic enterprise. Sometimes Emerson made warmly democratic statements that had Parker and George Bancroft (a quasi-Transcendentalist who was an active Jacksonian) in ecstasy (and had the Whigs wondering whether he was angling for a Custom House post); more often, though, he was severely critical of Jackson (whom he considered unfit to be President) and his followers and distrustful of mass politics. Only in the increase in the number of highly principled men and women did he see hope for social advance in the United States. He wanted an "a priori politics" of principle and a kind of ethical democracy.

Nevertheless, Emerson's thought was not wholly individualistic. The Kantian ethic which he wanted to guide people transcended both narrow self-interest and parochial concerns on the part of individuals. Emerson recognized that "the common good of all men" was a fundamental social consideration, favored equal opportunities for people from different classes, and praised the "generous ideas" of socialists like Robert Owen and Charles Fourier. He was troubled, too, by the development of extreme specialization in economic enterprise which he observed here and abroad. The machine, he feared, "unmans the user. What he gains in making cloth, he loses in general power. . . . The incessant repetition of the same hand-work dwarfs the man, robs him of his strength, wit and versatility, to make a pin polisher, a buckle-maker, or any other specialty." He thought an inordinate desire for wealth a symptom of mindlessness and on one occasion even said that whenever one person had no land the title of everybody else to land was "vitiated." He did defend private property in an argument with Thoreau, but it was clear that for him the test of private property, as of all social institutions, was its contribution to the moral development of individuals. For all his individualism, moreover, he was thoroughly community-minded. He loved the town of Concord where he spent most of his life, served many years on the school committee, and faithfully attended town meetings dealing with the questions of good roads, tax collections, and the disbursement of public money. And he was not entirely inactive in the larger public arena. He was

friendly to the feminist movement (though he had some
doubts about whether women should take an active role
in political life), and he made an address at a Women's
Rights Convention in 1855, in which he called for equal
educational opportunities and property rights for
women and demanded that "the law be purged of every
barbarous remainder, every barbarous impediment to
women." (In a day of exclusive gentlemen's clubs,
women like Margaret Fuller and Elizabeth Peabody participated freely in meetings of the Transcendental Club.)
He was aroused by the expulsion of the Cherokee Indians from their ancestral lands in Georgia and in 1838
wrote President Martin Van Buren a strongly worded
letter calling the U.S. Government "an instrument of
perfidy" and predicting that the name of the United
States "will stink to the world." (He had some misgivings
afterward for having been so outspoken.)

When it came to abolitionism, Emerson did not become passionately antislavery until after the passage of
the Fugitive Slave Act of 1850, but he did permit antislavery advocates to speak in Second Church, Boston,
while he was minister there, praised Elijah Lovejoy as a
hero in a public lecture in 1837 at a time when Boston
was still hostile to antislavery, and made a moving address in 1844 on behalf of black citizens from Massachusetts who had been seized on vessels lying in Southern ports. Until 1850, it is true, Emerson was decidedly
lukewarm about the antislavery movement. He had some
doubts about black ability at first, was put off by the
outspokenness of militant abolitionists, and, as a Transcendentalist, tended to stress slavery as a condition of
heart and mind rather than as a matter of external circumstances. (This line of reasoning made most whites
slaves, too, though it is unlikely that chattel slaves were
consoled by the point.) Still, by 1844, when he spoke in
Concord to celebrate the anniversary of emancipation in

the West Indies, he was friendlier than ever before toward the antislavery movement and had come to believe
that the facts about Negro life and behavior in the West
Indies and the United States refuted the "alleged hope-
less inferiority of the colored race." Yet for all his growing sympathy for reform, the reservations remained.
The individual should reform himself first. "I have not
yet conquered my own house," he mused, after refusing
to join Ripley at Brook Farm; "it irks and repents me.
Shall I raise the siege of this hen coop, and march baffled
away to a pretended siege of Babylon? It seems to me that
so to do were to dodge the problem." Moral education
was the only sure way to social amelioration. "What we
call our root-and-branch reforms of slavery, war, gam-
bling, intemperance," he said, "is only medicating the
symptoms. We must begin higher up, namely, in Education." The work of reformers, he continued to think, was
"done profanely, not piously; by management, by tactics
and clamor. It is a buzz in the ear." Nature surely
wouldn't have us fuss and fret so. "When we come out of
the caucus, or the bank, or the Transcendental club into
the fields and woods, she says to us, 'So hot, my little
Sir?' "

Thoreau and Civil Disobedience

Thoreau was even more aloof from social action than
Emerson until abolitionism swept him into its orbit; and
he spoke even more sharply than his older friend about
the mediocrity of men in the mass and the self-righteous
unctuousness of most professional reformers. "I am too
transcendental to serve you in your way," he told some
Temperance reformers; and he once remarked that it
was wiser to go to Mount Ktaadn in Maine than to a
women's rights or abolitionist convention. Like Emerson, he tended to equate moral with chattel slavery and

he once exclaimed: "It is hard to have a Southern over-
seer; it is worse to have a Northern one; but worst of all
when you are yourself the slave-driver." His view of
politics was even harsher than Emerson's. "What is called
politics is comparatively something so superficial and
inhuman," he cried, "that practically I have never fairly
recognized that it concerns me at all." He put the individual above the state and the individual's duty to follow
the highest dictate above all other duties. "There will
never be a really free and enlightened State," he said,

> until the State comes to recognize the individual as a
> higher and independent power, from which all its
> own power and authority are derived, and treats
> him accordingly. I please myself with imagining a
> State at last which can afford to be just to all men,
> and to treat the individual with respect as a neigh-
> bor; which even would not think it inconsistent with
> its own repose if a few were to live aloof from it, not
> meddling with it, nor embraced by it, who fulfilled
> all the duties of neighbors and fellow-man. A State
> which bore this kind of fruit, and suffered it to drop
> off as fast as it ripened, would prepare the way for a
> still more perfect and glorious State, which also I
> have imagined, but not yet anywhere seen.

But Thoreau recognized that the kind of arrangement
which he was imagining was a remote possibility. For the
time being, then, he was willing to offer the state a
Thoreauvian social contract: he would leave the state
alone if the state left him alone.

But the state would not leave Thoreau alone. In May,
1846, the U.S. Government declared war on Mexico,
proclaiming, as usual, response to aggression, but acting
(in the opinion of Thoreau and all antislavery New Englanders) under pressure from Southern planters to ex-

tend slavery into the Southwest. To protest against a state
which as part of the American Union supported slavery,
Thoreau had already stopped paying his Massachusetts
poll tax of $1.50 a year, four years earlier, but it was not
until the Mexican War began that local authorities decided to do something about it. He was arrested one
evening in July, 1846, spent the night in jail, and was
released the next morning only after his aunt (acting on
her own) paid the tax. If the government "requires you
to be the agent of injustice to another," Thoreau wrote
afterward, "then, I say, break the law." And he added:
"Under a government which imprisons any unjustly, the
true place for a just man is also a prison." There is an
apochryphal story to the effect that Emerson visited his
young friend in jail and asked, "Henry, why are you
there?" whereupon Thoreau exclaimed, "Why are you
not here?" The story is untrue but the point it makes is
valid. Emerson did have doubts about the propriety of
Thoreau's behavior, though Thoreau himself had no
doubts at all about the consonancy of his action with the
"higher law" that Transcendentalism urged as an
individual's moral guideline.

In a lecture "The Rights and Duties of the Individual
in Relation to Government," delivered early in 1849
(retitled "Civil Disobedience," when it was published
four years after his death), Thoreau reviewed his own
experience in jail briefly and explored at length the
implications of Transcendental higher law for citizen-
ship. He made it clear throughout that although he had
acted (and was prepared to act again) in protest against
slavery, he was in no sense a reformer. "I came into this
world," he explained, "not chiefly to make this a good
place to live in, but to live in it, be it good or bad." A few
years earlier he had gone to live in a hut he built on the
shores of Walden Pond in order to find out how life
would be, stripped down to a few essentials and spent in

close association with the natural environment. He left Walden because he had other lives to live, but who knows? Perhaps he would seek another Walden someday; at any rate, he fully intended further expeditions into the wilderness untroubled by social issues. "It is not a man's duty, as a matter of course," he declared, "to devote himself to the eradication of any, even the most enormous wrong; he may still properly have other concerns to engage him...." (But he added: "I must first see, at least, that I do not pursue them sitting upon another man's shoulders. I must get off him first, that he may pursue his contemplations too.") Thoreau thought an individual narrow indeed if he had no other concerns than reform. He did not think, moreover, that a conscientious individual was obliged to engage in continuous confrontation with the state, even though he might hold it in low esteem. Thoreau had refused to pay church taxes some years earlier and local officials had quite sensibly allowed him to "sign off" as a member of the church parish. But he had no objection to paying highway taxes, to supporting public schools, and to paying tariffs on goods imported from abroad, though he might have no use personally for any of these things. None of these activities involved higher moral law. But when a government tried to entangle an individual in unjust actions of its own, like sanctioning slavery, it was quite different. It was then the individual's "duty, at least, to wash his hands of it, and, if he gives it no thought longer, not to give it practically his support."

In presenting his case for civil disobedience, Thoreau carefully considered the alternatives: "Unjust laws exist: shall we be content to obey them, or shall we endeavor to amend them, and obey them until we have succeeded, or shall we transgress them at once?" For Thoreau, transgressing them at once was the only possible course of action for a Transcendentalist. To obey unjust laws was

unthinkable; but it was equally unthinkable for a moral
person to continue obeying unjust laws until it was possible to muster a majority of votes for repealing the unjust
laws. "Even voting *for the right*," Thoreau insisted, "is
doing nothing for it. It is only expressing to men feebly
your desire that it should prevail. A wise man will not
leave the right to the mercy of chance, nor wish it to
prevail through the power of majority. . . ." He firmly
rejected absolute majority rule. Majority rule, he said,
was based on strength, not justice, and while there was
nothing wrong with having majorities decide questions
to which the "rule of expediency" was applicable, it was
inconceivable to him that a citizen be obliged to surren-
der his conscience to majority opinion. "Why has every
man a conscience, then?" he asked. "I think that we
should be men first, and subjects afterwards. It is not
desirable to cultivate a respect for the law, so much as for
the right. The only obligation which I have a right to
assume is to do at any time what I think right." Thoreau
denied that he was a "no-government man"; he asked for
"not at once no government, but *at once* a better government." How was one to work for a better government?
By setting an example of highly principled behavior
whenever crucial moral issues, like slavery, were involved. There must be "some absolute goodness somewhere," Thoreau declared; "for that will leaven the
whole lump." Furthermore, action from principle was
"essentially revolutionary" and would have profound
effects on the attitudes and behavior of the majority.
Thoreau recommended that abolitionists in his part of
the country "at once effectually withdraw their support
both in person and property, from the government of
Massachusetts, and not wait till they constitute a majority
of one, before they suffer the right to prevail through
them."

Thoreau's essay on civil disobedience was in some ways

the most influential document of the Transcendental movement. Both Mohandas Gandhi and Martin Luther King testified to its profound influence on their lives and work, and leaders of the young British Labour party in the late nineteenth century also looked to it for inspiration. It is true that there have been vast changes in the American system since Thoreau's day—from the relatively easygoing Jeffersonianism that Thoreau knew to the implacable military Hamiltonianism of our own day—and that the conscientious objector today faces a much tougher situation than did Thoreau, who spent only a night in jail (though he would have been willing to stay longer). Still, the moral power of Thoreau's essay and his own moral courage in helping slaves escape to Canada and in publicly defending John Brown are undeniable, and there is no question of the importance of Thoreauvian principles in "leavening the whole lump" both here and abroad for more than a century.

Margaret Fuller and Women's Rights

Like Thoreau, Margaret Fuller also came to engage in civil disobedience, but it was in Italy, not America, and it involved supporting the Italian struggle for emancipation from foreign domination rather than emancipation of the blacks. By the time Thoreau wrote his celebrated essay, the "high-priestess of American Transcendentalism," as Brownson called her, had left Boston, where she had edited *The Dial*, for New York City, to become a writer for Horace Greeley's New York *Tribune*. Like Thoreau, Margaret Fuller was cool to reformers at first ("so tedious, often so narrow, always so rabid and exaggerated in their tone") and then found herself swept irresistibly into social action. Initially distrustful of abolitionists, she finally decided that they had "a high motive, something eternal in their desire and life" and that their efforts to free the United States from the terrible blot of slavery were entirely laudable. But her major interest at first was in self-culture, not reform, and she concentrated on literature rather than philosophy, though she was imbued with the philosophical idealism she encountered in German romantic literature. Her heroes were Goethe, Beethoven, Molière, Cervantes, and Shakespeare (as well as Emerson, whose *Nature* was her Bible for a time), her knowledge of Continental, especially German, literature prodigious, her aesthetic standards high, and her impatience with the spurious and second-rate barely concealable. Her father had been a severe taskmaster; when she was little he punished her for sneaking off to read Shakespeare instead of doing her lessons.

Emerson spoke of Margaret Fuller's "rather mountainous ME" and there were numerous stories about her intellectual vanity. (A favorite quotation has her remarking simply that she "never met her intellectual equal" in America and a famous story has her announcing, "I accept the universe," and Carlyle's snorting, "By Gad, she'd better!") But she had ample justification for self-esteem. She was a competent linguist and translator, an able teacher of languages in Alcott's Temple School in Boston, and even more accomplished as the leader of "Conversations" (informal lectures and discussions of ethical and aesthetic topics with audiences of twenty-five to thirty people) in Boston. She worked hard as editor of *The Dial*, 1840-1842, writing much of the material herself, and as literary critic for the New York *Tribune*, 1844-1846, she produced criticism of an exceedingly high order. She was, with Edgar Allan Poe, the best American literary critic of her day, and her estimates of her literary contemporaries hold up surprisingly well today.

But if literature was Margaret Fuller's first love, it was

in the field of reform that she made her most enduring contribution. In July, 1843, she published a long essay in *The Dial* entitled "The Great Lawsuit. Man versus Men. Woman versus Women," which she went on to expand into a book with the more felicitous title *Woman in the Nineteenth Century* (1845). In her book, which became popular among feminists, she took a Transcendental view of woman: If the creative vitality women possess were permitted free expression, "the divine energy would pervade nature to a degree unknown in the history of former ages." Margaret Fuller was interested in vocation rather than voting (and for this reason her book dropped out of circulation when American feminists, later on, began concentrating on the suffrage). "What woman needs," she said, "is not as a woman to act or rule, but as a nature to grow, as an intellect to discern, as a soul to live freely and unimpeded, to unfold such powers as were given her when we left our common home." Penelope, she said, was no more meant to be a baker or weaver than Ulysses to be a cattle herder, but as to women's occupations, "if you ask me what offices they may fill, I reply—any. I do not care what case you put; let them be sea captains, if you will." (Greeley used to exclaim, "LET THEM BE SEA CAPTAINS IF THEY WILL," whenever Margaret Fuller waited for him to open the door for her.) Woman was to have "inward and outward freedom" as a right not a concession, and she was to discover her destiny without the advice of man, though she might teach him how to aid her. For the time being, Margaret Fuller decided, women were "the best helpers of one another" in discovering themselves. "Let them think; let them act; till they know what they need. We only ask of men to remove arbitrary barriers." But man, she said, should learn to think of himself as friend and brother, not as lord and master of women.

Give the soul free course, let the organization both of body and mind be freely developed, and the being will be fit for any and every relation to which it may be called. The intellect, no more than the sense of hearing, is to be cultivated merely that Woman may be a more valuable companion to Man, but because the Power who gave a power by its mere existence signifies that it must be brought out toward perfection.

The tone of *Woman in the Nineteenth Century* was too literary and philosophical to please militant feminists entirely, but they welcomed it as a contribution to the cause (while respectable people excoriated the book), and it played some part in shaping the feminine "Declaration of Independence" issued by the Seneca Falls Conference in 1848. The book was also noticed in England. When Margaret Fuller arrived in London in 1846, on a grand tour of Europe as foreign correspondent for Greeley's *Tribune*, she found she was well-known because of her book. In England she met Carlyle, Wordsworth, and De Quincey, in France George Sand and Frédéric Chopin, and in Italy she met, fell in love with, and married a young Italian nobleman who belonged to a revolutionary party called Young Italy, which was struggling for Italian independence from Austria. Margaret Fuller was soon swept up into the revolutionary movement, working in hospitals when Rome was under siege and pleading for American sympathy for the Roman revolution in the columns of the *Tribune*. When the revolution was put down by French troops she sailed for the United States with her husband and child, but all three perished in a shipwreck off the shore of Fire Island, New York, in July, 1850. By the close of her career Margaret Fuller had become the most cosmopolitan of all the Transcendentalists through her Italian experience, and she had come to have doubts about creative living in the United States. Before the collapse of the revolution, when friends had pressed her to return to America calling it the "land of the future," she had replied:

> It is so, but that spirit which made it all it is of value in my eyes, which gave all of hope with which I can sympathize for the future, is more alive here at present than in America. My country is at present spoiled by prosperity, stupid with the lust of gain, soiled by crime in its willing perpetuation of slavery, shamed by an unjust war. . . . In Europe, amid the teachings of adversity, a nobler spirit is struggling—a spirit which cheers and animates mine.

Alcott, the Temple School, and Fruitlands

Margaret Fuller and Henry Thoreau came to reform gradually and with some reluctance. Bronson Alcott, a self-educated farm boy, was a reformer from the beginning. A Connecticut schoolmaster who had peddled trinkets in the South for a while and come under Quaker influence there, Alcott arrived in Boston in 1828 with definite ideas on how to reform the world: through educating the young. Commonly regarded as the most Transcendental of all the Transcendentalists, Alcott developed a philosophy that went much further in the direction of idealism than any of his associates were prepared to go, though Emerson was impressed with Alcott's ideas and even used some of them in his essays. Alcott thought that man was a projection of Universal Spirit (as all the Transcendentalists did) and that nature was a projection of man, or "Man in ruins" (which no other Transcendentalist did, except in the sense that

man's mind shapes his perception of the natural world).
He also took up Plato's doctrine of the preexistence of
human souls in a spiritual realm before birth and held
that since human beings emanated from Universal
Spirit, young children, who had emanated most recently,
were closer to divinity than adults, their minds less
clouded by the imperfections of the mundane world, and
their ability to grasp spiritual truth, through intuition,
more acute than that of most older people. Education,
then, should be directed to the very young, and it should
be centered on drawing out of them the moral and
spiritual truths latent in the intuitive Reason they all
possess. Alcott was convinced that with Socratic methods
it would be possible to elicit all the ideas of Plato from a
group of twenty properly chosen youngsters. He also
thought that all children were created equal, in terms of
moral and intellectual potentiality, and that circumstantial contingencies (which education might overcome)
were responsible for inequalities in achievement. Later
on, he came to appreciate the powerful force of heredity
in shaping human beings and even became interested in
genealogy, but he never abandoned his Transcendental
faith in the divine possibilities of all men and women.

Alcott was both shrewd and visionary. His judgment of
people and events was remarkably perceptive at times;
his educational theory, stressing the organic growth of
the child and his close relation to the natural and social
environments, was carefully conceived and surprisingly
modern. But the more outlandish aspects of his idealism,
especially when expounded in his frequently flatulent
prose, attracted ridicule even among Transcendentalists. "Since Plato and Plotinus we have not had his
like," Emerson told a friend; he was "a large piece of
spiritual New England." But Emerson also remarked
that sometimes Alcott seemed like "a tedious archangel, a
pail of which the bottom is out." Carlyle called him "a

venerable Don Quixote, who nobody can laugh at without loving," but was bored stiff by his idealistic pronouncements. Alcott's *Orphic Sayings*, which appeared from time to time in *The Dial*, reminded one critic of "a train of fifteen coaches going by, with only one passenger." Ripley grumbled that Alcott lacked a sense of humor. Parker once asked him to define his terms. "Only God defines," said Alcott, "man can but confine." "Well, then," rejoined Parker, "please confine." But Alcott did confine when he thought it appropriate. Despite his reputation for discarding all discipline for spontaneity, he carefully organized the classroom and required full attention and good behavior on the part of the pupils at all times. He did, however, discard rote memory, common in his day, and concentrate on encouraging the natural development of the child's interest in the materials of geography, arithmetic, and grammar. Some of his techniques resembled those of the great Swiss educator Henry Pestalozzi, with whom Alcott was familiar, and he was frequently called "the American Pestalozzi." But Alcott's methods were largely his own.

In 1834, Alcott opened a school for thirty pre-teen-age boys and girls in the Masonic Temple in Boston, with Elizabeth Peabody (geography) and Margaret Fuller (languages) as his assistants. There were separate desks and blackboards for the children, busts of Milton, Shakespeare, Socrates, and Plato in the corners of the room, and a bas-relief of Jesus by Alcott's desk. Alcott read stories and poems to the children, conducted discussions about them, often centering on the meaning of words, and encouraged the older pupils to keep journals in which they recorded the ideas that came to them each day. There were exercise periods for the youngsters, for Alcott was aware of the active nature of children, and there were efforts to develop a "common conscience" in the classroom by having all the students participate in the selection of punishments for unruly individuals. For the misdeeds of one child, Alcott frequently saw to it that the whole class was punished (perhaps by omitting readings) and sometimes he even had himself punished (by having the miscreant strike him) in order to demonstrate the social effects of individual misbehavior. In addition to readings and discussions, Alcott loved to conduct "Conversations" designed to draw out, by the Socratic method, the basic truths which he thought lay in the recesses of every child's mind; he was disarmingly unaware of the Alcottian quality of most of his pupils' responses. In the fall of 1835, he began a series of "Conversations" on the Christian Gospel which Elizabeth Peabody and her sister Sophia (who later married Nathaniel Hawthorne) faithfully recorded and which Alcott decided to publish. Just before publication, Elizabeth Peabody had misgivings and begged Alcott to eliminate some of the material—especially that having to do with the birth of Jesus—which she thought might offend some readers. Alcott obligingly cut the objectionable passages out of the text and relegated them to an appendix marked "Omitted by Recorder." When *Record of Conversations on the Gospel* (2 volumes, 1836-37) reached the public, a storm broke. Not only did Boston clergymen consider Alcott a "theological interloper" for discussing religion (and transcendentally at that) in the classroom; they were also shocked by one particular passage appearing in the appendix:

> And a mother suffers when she has a child. When she is going to have a child she gives up her body to God and He works upon it in a mysterious way and, with her aid, brings forth the child's Spirit in a little Body of its own; and when it has come she is blissful.

The Boston *Daily Advertiser* called the book "indecent and

obscene" and predicted "mischievous effects" from it, the Boston *Courier* ran a piece accusing Alcott of trying to "pollute the moral atmosphere" of the city and urged legal action, and Andrews Norton was quoted as saying of the book that "one-third was absurd, one-third blasphemous, and one-third obscene." James F. Clarke defended the book in a letter to the *Christian Register* and praised it in the *Western Messenger*, and Brownson also came to Alcott's defense in the *Boston Quarterly Review*, a journal he had just founded. Emerson wrote the *Courier*, exclaiming, "Let the book be read," and he also wrote the *Advertiser* a letter which the editor refused to print. To Alcott, Emerson wrote: "I hate to have all the little dogs barking at you, for you have something better to do than attend to them. . . ." But the Temple School rapidly declined in enrollment following the newspaper attacks, and Alcott was finally forced to sell the school furniture and books and move what was left of the class to his home in Boston. A few months later, when he took a black girl into the school, everyone withdrew except his own daughters, and he was forced to close the school.

Alcott was disappointed but undaunted. If he could not save the world in the classroom, perhaps he could do so in a Transcendental community made up of people who lived simply, naturally, and nobly, and by their example encouraged the rest of the world to do the same. Emerson helped finance a trip to England (Alcott was perennially penniless) to visit Alcott House, a school in Richmond modeled after the Temple School, and there Alcott met Charles Lane, a Transcendental English journalist, who offered to invest his savings in an enterprise in America that might set in motion the regeneration of all society. Returning to the United States with Lane and Lane's young son, Alcott arranged for the purchase of a ninety-acre farm near the village of Harvard, thirty miles south of Boston, and in June, 1843,

launched a community which he called "Fruitlands."
Fruitlands was the tiniest of all the experimental colonies
appearing in the United States in the 1840's; it never
attracted more than a handful of people besides the five
Alcotts and the two Lanes. Nevertheless, Alcott took his
calling as a "Paradise Planter" with utmost seriousness
and though he stressed cooperative individualism rather
than communal coercion, the prohibitions—against enslaving animals or using any products resulting from the
enslaving of animals or men—were so extensive that
most of the time the colonists were reduced to eating
cornmeal mush and wearing linen clothing. "The pure
soul. . . ," Alcott explained,

> adopts a pure diet and cleanly customs. . . . The
> greater part of man's duty consists in leaving alone
> much that he is in the habit of doing. Shall I sip tea or
> coffee? . . . No. Abstain from all ardent, as from
> alcoholic drinks. Shall I consume pork, beef or
> mutton? No, if you value health or life. Shall I stimu-
> late with milk? No. Shall I warm my bathing water?
> Not if cheerfulness is valuable. Shall I prolong my
> dark morning, consuming animal oil, and losing
> bright daylight in the morning? Not if a clear mind is
> an object. . . . Shall I become a hireling, or hire
> others? Shall I subjugate cattle? Shall I trade? Shall I
> claim property in any created things? . . . To
> how many of these questions, could we ask deeply
> enough . . . would the response be—"Ab-
> stain. Be not so active to do as sincere to Be."

The Fruitlanders were indeed more sincere than active.
Though a union of labor and leisure was the theme of the
community, there were always more conversations than
crops. Except for Mrs. Alcott, who did the best she could
with the harvesting, the colonists turned out to be poor

farmers. "There was only one slave at Fruitlands," she later remarked, "and that was a woman." Emerson was amused by the undertaking: "They look well in July," he confided to his journal; "we shall see them in December." He was right; by December the experiment in "spiritual culture" had come to an end. Lane, who had been unhappily married in England, proposed abolishing the family (along with private property and government), and Alcott, after a severe emotional crisis, chose his family over a celibate community. At this point, Lane, who had suspected all along that the Transcendentalists were hedonists, went off to join the celibate Shakers and then in the spring returned to England where he eventually remarried. Meanwhile another member of Alcott's colony, Joseph Palmer, "the Man with the Beard," bought Fruitlands and for a while he and his wife provided a refuge there for the poor and hungry. (For refusing to shave, Palmer for years suffered ridicule, intimidation, repeated assault, and lengthy imprisonment, and he was a virtual outcast until after the Civil War, when whiskers became fashionable. He died in 1875 and his gravestone read: "Persecuted for Wearing the Beard.") The failure of Alcott's experiment in high-minded Transcendental living caused him considerable anguish, but he eventually snapped out of it, found a vocation in conducting "Conversations" throughout the Northeast and Middle West and, as his daughter Louisa May observed, did "as well as a philosopher can in a money-loving world."

Ripley and Brook Farm

George Ripley did considerably better at Brook Farm than Alcott did at Fruitlands, though Alcott said Ripley's project was "not sufficiently ideal." Ripley had resigned his Boston pulpit in the fall of 1840 because he thought the purpose of Christianity was "to redeem society as well as the individual from all sin," and in the spring of 1841 he organized a joint stock company and raised money enough to purchase a farm of 160 acres in West Roxbury, a few miles from Boston, where he founded the Brook Farm Institute for Education and Agriculture. Brook Farm, which started with about twenty members and came to average about seventy, was a cooperative community made up mainly of teachers, students, and workers (farmhands, urban laborers, and craftsmen), who operated three schools, engaged in farming, gardening, and light industries, and sold their surplus products at the nearest market. All the Brook Farmers ate in a communal dining hall, did both physical and intellectual work, received the same wages, and could attend the schools free of charge. But private property was retained (though competition was eliminated), and there were houses for individual families as well as dormitories for single people. "Our objects. . . ," Ripley told Emerson,

> are to insure a more natural union between intellectual and manual labor than now exists; to combine the thinker and the worker, as far as possible, in the same individual; to guarantee the highest mental freedom, by providing all with labor, adapted to their tastes and talents, and securing to them the fruits of their industry, to do away with the necessity of menial services, by opening the benefits of education and the profits of labor to all; and thus to prepare a society of liberal, intelligent, and cultivated persons, whose relations with each other would permit a more simple and wholesome life, than can be led amidst the pressure of our competitive institutions.

Emerson could not be persuaded to join, nor did any of the other Transcendentalists become members of the community, except Dwight, though they took a keen interest in it and visited it frequently. Though Thoreau grumbled that he would rather "keep bachelor's hall in hell than go to board in heaven, if that place is heaven," Emerson good-naturedly called it "a perpetual picnic, a French Revolution in small, an Age of Reason in a patty-pan."

Emerson erred in calling Brook Farm a perpetual picnic. Nathaniel Hawthorne, who lived there a few months, found he was too tired to write after chopping hay, carrying wood, piling manure, and milking cows, though Ripley himself found milking cows favorable to contemplation, *"particularly when the cow's tail was looped up behind."* But there was play as well as work —charades, dances, theatricals, concerts, readings, pageants, games, and lively discussions at all times—and Hawthorne, despite his criticisms and a quarrel, later, with Ripley over money, looked back on his Brook Farm experience as the most romantic episode in his life and used it as a background for *The Blithedale Romance* (1852). The community was "rich in cheerful buzz" all the time and sometimes, led by Ripley, an archpunster, rich in outrageous puns. "Mr. Ripley, Mr. Ripley," exclaimed a member one day, "I am perfectly happy." The community attracted great attention and many visitors, and during one year more than four thousand people came to observe. They were amazed by the dress adopted by many of the Brook Farmers: the men's peasant tunics, Byron collars, sack trousers, boots, visored caps, long hair, and beards; and the women's short skirts, knickerbockers, long flowing coiffeurs, and wide-brimmed hats adorned with vines, berries, and flowers. People like Emerson, Alcott, Brownson, Hedge, Margaret Fuller, and Elizabeth Peabody came more than once and were all impressed by the joyous combination of labor and culture they encountered and especially by the educational program: the infant and primary schools, the three-year agricultural course, and the six-year college preparatory course. Both Ripley and his wife, Sophia, taught as well as worked, as did all the other instructors, and their pupils worked as well as studied. Brownson praised the community for operating on the assumption that "true democratic equality may be obtained by *levelling* up, instead of *levelling* down."

In 1844, Ripley, won over to the ideas of Charles Fourier, French socialist (1772-1837), through the promptings of Albert Brisbane (Fourier's chief American disciple), decided to Fourierize Brook Farm. This meant following the specifications for proper community organizing laid down in Brisbane's *The Social Destiny of Man* (1840), a lengthy (and at times deadly) exposition of Fourier's major proposals. Fourier emphasized "attractive industry": seeing to it that people did the kind of work they most enjoyed doing. Each individual, according to Fourier, possessed a variety of passions requiring satisfaction, and there was no job, however repellent it might be to some people, that other people wouldn't mind doing. (Children liked to play in the dirt, Fourier noticed, so why not have them collect garbage, clean sewers, and spread manure?) The trick in organizing a thoroughly integrated and harmonious society (and thus eliminating the class struggle that so distressed Fourier) lay in providing each individual in it with a variety of tasks and personal associations at work to which he was naturally drawn by the "law of passional attraction." (Fourier also favored variety in sexual as well as work relations, with a minimum of sexual pleasure guaranteed all citizens, but Brisbane discreetly omitted this aspect of Fourierism from his book.) The basic unit in Fourier's scheme was the "phalanx," a small, self-sufficient community of about 1,600 people (representing all the different varieties of human nature), occupying three square miles of land, in the center of which was a huge, three-story phalanstery, containing living quarters, kitchens, dining rooms, and workshops. The phalanx itself was organized into Series (Agricultural, Mechanical, and Domestic Industry), and each Series was divided into Groups of about seven people each. In the Farming Series there were Planting, Ploughing, Hoeing, and Weeding Groups in the fields, Cattle and Milking Groups in the barns, and Nursery and Greenhouse Groups to attend to gardening. The Mechanical and Domestic Series were similarly subdivided. Since each member of the phalanx belonged to thirty or forty groups of his own choosing, moving freely from one to the other and spending only an hour or two in each, there was no reason why he should not be happy at work. By advocating a division of labor based on individual talents and on the passion for variety and pleasant associations, Fourier hoped to end the worker's alienation from his work; by providing community life in the phalanstery, he hoped to end the fragmentation of modern life and develop social solidarity. He figured out that there should be 2,000,000 phalanxes in the world and that when people were thoroughly Fourierized they would grow to be ten feet tall, live three or four hundred years, and produce thousands of poets like Homer, scientists like Newton, and writers like Molière. In Americanizing Fourier, Brisbane omitted some of his nuttier notions, but hostile Americans referred to Fourierites as "Furyites" anyway.

Though some of Fourier's ideas—especially his suggestions for making work more satisfying and socializing the atomized individual of modern industrial society —impressed Marx and Engels and are of continuing interest, the conversion of Brook Farm into a phalanx was probably an error and helped shorten the life of the community. Ripley adopted Fourierism because he thought Brook Farm needed a basic philosophy and plan of organization if it was to endure and because he wanted to link his experiment with communitarian experiments going on elsewhere. He thought, too, that Transcendentalism and Fourierism had much in common: the desire to have people express themselves freely and honestly, not compulsively, at work and play; and the wish to keep modern economic life from transforming them into work-machines and profit-lovers. But he overlooked another equally important Transcendental principle when he went over to Fourierism: that form and organization cannot be artificially imposed on a community from the outside but must grow naturally out of the needs and aspirations of the people themselves.

With the coming of Fourierism, the free inquiry, mutual tolerance, and joyous spontaneity that had made Brook Farm so attractive declined rapidly and in their place came long, pompous lectures by Brisbane, interminable discussions of Groups and Series, and elaborate preparations for celebrating Fourier's birthday. The "law of Groups and Series" may have been the "law of human nature," as the organizers of the Brook Farm Phalanx asserted in January, 1844, but surely talking solemnly about organization all the time was not. Ripley now gave lectures on Fourier instead of on Kant and Spinoza, as had been his former custom, and he tried to Fourierize the classroom with detailed rules and regular study hours. Pedantry replaced poetry at Brook Farm; and the schools, the former community's most striking achievement, lost their spirit as members bent all their energies to creating a perfect phalanx. On one visit to the new phalanx, Parker saw one of the phalangists running around wildly, crying: "Oh! The pigs have got into the cornfield, and I am looking for the Miscellaneous Group to drive them out." There was a story, too, fabricated by outsiders, no doubt, of the young Brook Farmer who refused to dig potatoes because he belonged to the "eating group." Emerson decided that Fourier "had skipped no fact but one, namely Life," and the Transcendentalists stopped visiting the community. One evening in March, 1846, a fire destroyed the big phalanstery which the Brook Farmers had been working on for many months and the heart seems to have gone out of the community after that. The following year the place was abandoned. Like Alcott, Ripley was bitterly disappointed at the failure of his enterprise, and, though he left Boston to take a job in New York on Greeley's *Tribune* and never tried community building again, he continued to assert his belief in Fourier's principles. "The work of ages goes on," he declared; "man advances nearer to the freedom which is his birthright."

Brownson as Social Critic

While he was still at Brook Farm, Ripley reproached his friend Brownson for not supporting his community more enthusiastically. "If I had never known you," he wrote him in December, 1842, "I should never have engaged in this enterprise." He told Brownson that he regarded Brook Farm as the "incarnation of those transcendental truths" which the two held in common and that a friendly word from Brownson would cheer him immensely. Brownson did visit Brook Farm; he also praised its schools as the best he had ever observed, and he sent his son there for a year. But he did not share Ripley's hope that experimental communities like Brook Farm would point the way to general reform. He also disagreed with the Transcendental belief that moral regeneration of the individual paved the way for social reform, though he had once held this view himself. Brownson was unique among Transcendentalists: he was interested in realistic social action and for a time associated himself with the Jacksonian Democrats in the struggle against privilege. Brownson was noted for his "gladiatorial vigor." He threw himself wholeheartedly into whatever cause captured his sympathy, having moved successively from Calvinistic Presbyterianism to Universalism, agnosticism, Unitarianism, and then to Transcendentalism. In 1836, he organized an independent congregation in Boston called the Society for Christian Union and Progress, dedicated to religious and social reform, which he hoped would become the "Church of the Future." In 1838, he founded the *Boston Quarterly Review* in which to expound his increasingly radical social views. Like all the Transcendentalists he had originally believed that there was "no such thing as reforming the mass without reforming the individuals who compose it." The Panic of 1837 and the harrowing depression that followed it forced Brownson to reexamine his views. With people starving, he asked, was it proper to concentrate on saving their souls? "Perfect all your men, and no doubt, you could then perfect easily and safely your institutions," he declared. "But when all your men are perfect, what need of perfecting your institutions? And wherein are those institutions, under which all individuals may attain to the full perfection admitted by human nature, imperfect?" Influenced by his reading of Fourier, Saint-Simon, and other early European socialists, Brownson began to see history as the story of class struggle. In Europe, the struggle was between nobles and merchants, but in America, which had no feudal past, the clash was between merchants and laborers. Brownson began to see the Democratic party as the party of the people and the Whigs as the party of privilege, and in the late 1830's, urged on by George Bancroft, he joined the Democratic party.

Brownson never got entirely away from the habit of individuating social evil; nor do most people even today.

Like all Jacksonian Democrats, he tended to blame the ills of the land on greedy bankers and monopolists rather than on the kind of impersonal system that modern industry and technology were producing. Yet he did arrive at a realistic view of the social process (unusual for an American in his day) and a keen grasp of the social context of individual behavior. When it came to specifics, he took the Jacksonian view: internal improvements, protective tariffs, and the Second Bank of the United States were devices by which the Whigs, representing privilege, took government away from the people and lodged it in the hands of monopolists. The task of reformers lay in wresting control of government from special business interests; and their first immediate responsibility was to support the Democratic candidate Martin Van Buren over the Whig candidate William Henry Harrison in the presidential campaign of 1840. In the *Boston Quarterly Review* for July, 1840, Brownson published the first installment of his sensational two-part essay "The Laboring Classes," in which his social radicalism reached its high-water mark. In it, he unequivocally condemned the wage system by which the few exploited the many, blamed the social order, not its managers, for social evil, called for radical changes in social arrangements leading to social and economic equality for all men, and aligned himself with the "proletaries" in what he called the "new struggle" between wealth and labor.

There must be no class of our fellow men doomed to toil through life as mere workmen at wages. If wages are tolerated it must be, in the case of the individual operative, only under such conditions that by the time he is of a proper age to settle in life, he shall have accumulated enough to be an independent laborer on his own capital—on his own farm or in his own shop. Here is our work. How is it to be done?

How indeed? Brownson's proposals for reform, though directed to achieving laissez-faire in almost its purest form in America, seemed radical to his contemporaries, and have a radical ring even today. He called for abolishing the priestly office, reviving the "Christianity of Christ," freeing government (both federal and state) from banking control, repealing all antilabor laws and replacing them with laws guaranteeing the equality of the laboring classes, and strictly limiting the powers of government in order to prevent their abuse by the business community. (Brownson's preference was for laissez-faire and states' rights, because he thought that a strong central government inevitably becomes an instrument of privilege.) His most radical proposal—it still seems so today—was for the abolition of hereditary property, "the privilege which some have of being born rich while others are born poor," which he described as the greatest of all privileges and the most powerful of all monopolies. "A man shall have all he honestly requires," said Brownson,

> so long as he himself belongs to the world in which he acquires it. But his power over his property must cease with his life, and his property must then become the property of the state, to be disposed of by some equitable law for the use of the generation which takes his place.

Brownson realized that it would not be easy to abolish the hereditary descent of property; he doubted, in fact, whether abolition would come about without a social war, "the like of which the world has yet never witnessed." But he stuck to his guns. Ignoring the angry cries that greeted his proposals, he resumed his argument for them in the October issue of his journal and repeated his forecast of a terrible "social war" in the world at large, "a war between two social elements, between the aristocracy and the democracy, between the people and their masters." The Whigs, expectably, made extensive use of Brownson's articles in the campaign of 1840 to prove that the Democrats were dangerous radicals and the Democrats themselves hastily disavowed Brownson's views. But the victory of the Whigs in the 1840 election seems to have shattered Brownson's faith in the people and he gradually receded from the radicalism of "The Laboring Classes." His inclinations toward laissez-faire and states' rights led him for a time into alliance with John C. Calhoun (whom he pushed for the presidency in 1844), and he became steadily more conservative in outlook. In point of fact, though, his disillusionment with the possibilities of politics after 1840 was leading him rapidly away from a concern for social reform to a renewal of interest in religion. In 1844, he repudiated his Transcendental past *in toto* and joined the Catholic church.

The Transcendentalists and Abolitionism

Most of the Transcendentalists did not know quite what to make of Brownson's political and social views, and they were even more puzzled by his conversion to Catholicism. But Parker was impressed by "The Laboring Classes" and, although he had doubts about abolishing hereditary property, acknowledged that "the present property system entails awful evils upon society, rich no less than poor. This question," he decided, "first, of inherited property, and, next, of all private property, is to be handled in the nineteenth century." Parker became an indefatigable reformer after moving from West Roxbury to Boston in 1845. He served on reform committees, circulated petitions on behalf of good causes, organized charitable and welfare societies, and took an interest in every social problem of the day: alcoholism, women's rights, capital punishment, crime, prostitution, and prisons. He even borrowed some of Brownson's ideas, attacked the "feudalism of money" in his sermons, and declared that the exploitation of labor in the North was only one remove from slavery in the South. But like all the Transcendentalists, he relied on moral regeneration rather than social reconstruction for progress. He was deeply democratic; one of his favorite phrases, "government *of* all, *by* all, and *for* all," eventually caught Abraham Lincoln's eye. He was also sanguine in his hopes for the future; when millennialist William Miller predicted the Second Coming of Christ for October 22, 1843, he groaned, "Too long to wait!" But he lacked the social perceptions of Brownson at his best, and he remained essentially a moralist despite his growing awareness of the social setting for personal ethics.

In the 1850's, abolitionism became Parker's greatest cause, and he joined William Lloyd Garrison and Wendell Phillips in their campaign to abolitionize the North. The passage of the Fugitive Slave Act in September, 1850, galvanized Parker into action, and it also made militant abolitionists out of the other leading Transcendentalists. To the Transcendentalists, it seemed inconceivable that Northerners with any sense of decency would permit black people who had risked their lives for freedom to be sent back into slavery. Emerson called the law "a filthy enactment" and exclaimed, "I will not obey it, by God." Thoreau and Alcott, who had sheltered fugitive slaves even before passage of the law, were similarly resolved on civil disobedience. Parker not only helped conceal fugitive slaves; he also served on a Vigilance Committee formed to protect fugitives in Boston from seizure by the authorities, helped hound "slave-hunters" out of town, prepared inflammatory placards to rouse Bostonians against enforcement of the law, and even took part (as did Alcott) in an attempt in May, 1854, to rescue Anthony Burns, fugitive from Virginia, from the Court House where he was confined. When the effort failed and Burns was sent back to Virginia, Thoreau announced in Framingham in his speech "Slavery in Massachusetts": "My thoughts are murder to the State, and involuntarily go plotting against her." Parker, known as "Reverend Thunder and Lightning" because of his fiery abolition sermons, was eventually indicted by a grand jury for his part in the Burns case, energetically prepared a long brief to use in court, and was disappointed when the indictment was quashed on technicalities.

When John Brown came to Boston looking for help in his Kansas activities, he impressed all the Transcendentalists by his dedication to principle, and they gave him both moral and financial support. By this time Parker was convinced that only force would free the slaves and that a slave insurrection was fully justified. Emerson still hoped for some kind of compensated emancipation, but Thoreau was beginning to think that there were circumstances in which "to kill or be killed" would be unavoidable. Harper's Ferry took them all by surprise (though Parker knew that Brown intended to invade the South sooner or later), but they all hailed Brown as a hero, a martyr, and a saint. In "A Plea for Captain John Brown," in the Concord town hall on October 30, 1859, Thoreau made the first public defense of Brown in the country; he called the Harper's Ferry raid "the best news that America has ever heard" and said Brown was "a transcendentalist, above all, a man of ideas and principles." In his "Plea," Thoreau acknowledged that most Americans applauded the use of weapons in duels, quarrels with other nations, and against fugitive slaves, but he, for his part, preferred Brown's use of them. "I think that for once the Sharp's rifles and the revolvers were employed in a righteous cause." On the day of Brown's execution, he organized a memorial service for him, in which Emerson and Alcott took part, and the following day helped one of Brown's men, who had escaped at Harper's Ferry, on his way to Canada. From Rome, where he had gone for his health, Parker wrote to praise Brown's heroism and to regret that he had not been at home to defend "the True and the Right." The Transcendentalists had come to feel about slavery much as American liberals did about Nazism a century later.

Though antislavery sentiment increased enormously in the Boston area in the late 1850's, there were still many people there who were appalled by the direction in which abolitionism was moving. By helping fugitive slaves to escape, they asserted, Transcendentalists like Parker were openly flouting the law of the land and promoting general lawlessness and anarchy. Parker responded to criticism of this nature by calling attention to the selective enforcement of the law in Massachusetts. While the authorities were zealous in enforcing the Fugitive Slave Law, he observed, they blandly ignored the violation of many other laws. "How many laws of Massachusetts," he demanded to know, "have been violated this very week, in this very city, by the slave-hunters here, by the very officers of the State?" Parker's general impression was that every law "which favours the accumulation of money must be kept, but those which prohibit the unjust accumulation of money—by certain classes—they need not be kept." (The Transcendentalists also remembered that when he was President, Jackson had ignored a ruling of the U.S. Supreme Court in favor of the Cherokee Indians of Georgia in 1835 and that he had sought, in contravention of the Bill of Rights, Congressional legislation prohibiting the circulation of antislavery literature in the South.) Parker denied that the Transcendentalists were lawless in any fundamental sense; they were willing to obey any law (even those they disapproved) that did not violate the Higher Law. "If we do not obey this law (it is said) we shall disobey all laws," Parker noted.

> It is not so. There is not a country in the world where there is more respect for human laws than in New England, nowhere more than in Massachusetts. Even if a law is unpopular, it is not popular to disobey it. . . . Who is it that oppose the fugitive slave law? Men that have always been on the side of law and order and do not violate the statutes of man for their own advantage. This disobedience to the fugitive slave law is one of the strongest guarantees for the observance of any *just* law. You cannot trust a people who will keep a law *because it is law*; nor need we distrust a people that will only keep a law when it is just.

How was one to be sure he was right when he took the momentous step into civil disobedience? Parker—and the other Transcendentalists—thought the answer to this question was obvious. Like all Transcendentalists, Parker looked to his intuitive Reason, source of all basic truth and goodness, to discover what was right. And his Reason made it clear that black people, like all people, possessed something of the Divine Spirit within them and that slavery was a monstrous violation of the divine right they shared with all human beings to freedom and self-development. "Because every man has within him somewhat really divine," said Emerson, "therefore is slavery the unpardonable outrage it is."

But what if one were not a Transcendentalist? And what if, furthermore, one believed, as John C. Calhoun did, that blacks were inferior, morally and mentally, to whites and that slavery was a just and proper means for integrating them into American life? If Parker could engage in civil disobedience on behalf of his Transcendental principles, could not Calhoun practice nullification (even secession) to support his particular views of what was right and true? Parker answered this question when he pointed out that those who violated the Fugitive Slave Law did not do so "for their own advantage"; their motivation (unlike the slaveholders') was principle, not self-interest, the principle that all human beings were spiritually equal. How could one be sure this principle was valid? For the Transcendentalists, belief in this principle was too deep-seated to be argued about; it was a moral insight into the human condition possessing unquestioned validity. From the Transcendental point of view, those who did not accept it were simply closing their minds to the intuitions of Reason. They were also betraying the faith in equal human rights proclaimed by that semi-Transcendental document the Declaration of Independence and ignoring the Kantian rule that one should not treat people in ways (e.g., slavery) that one was not prepared to make universal. Spiritual equality was a religious affirmation for the Transcendentalists, not an analytical proposition. To deny it, said Parker, was "practical atheism."

What the Parker-Calhoun rift came down to, from a secular point of view, was two clashing sets of values and two divergent views of the good society: one based on faith in human possibilities, equal opportunities, individual freedom, and social mobility; the other based on inequality, privilege, hierarchy, and social stratification in its most rigid form. For the Transcendentalists the choice between the two was obvious, but it was also obvious for slaveholders like Calhoun. In the end, the American people made their choice between the two during the Civil War. The majority (which Thoreau distrusted) won the case against slavery on the battlefield; but it was a majority that included many people who did not share Thoreau's or Parker's Transcendental idealism. But the Transcendentalists were unaware of these ironies, inherent in all human situations; nor were they bothered by the facts that the war required the kind of bureaucratic organization which they detested and that the organized killing it involved violated high principle, even though it was fought, from another point of view, on behalf of high principle. That two equally high principles (for example, peace and freedom) may clash in actual practice seems not to have occurred to the Transcendentalists. Nor did it ever occur to them that good might come from evil and evil from good. The fact, moreover, that human choices are usually morally ambiguous, not self-evidently valid and not based on simple distinctions between good and evil, also escaped them. This was not so much due to their lack of sophistication as to their meliorative view of the historical process and their belief that there were no problems that would not, in the long run, work themselves out. They supported the Union cause with dedication and fervor and saw the Civil War as a gigantic contest between freedom and slavery, out of which would come a cleaner, healthier, wiser, and more principled America. Their faith in the redemptive power of the war was powerful. For the Transcendentalists, the Civil War was another step—a colossal one—on the road to human betterment. Their hopes for the future were unbounded. Their optimism had cosmic proportions.

CHAPTER FIVE

Cosmic Optimism

THOMAS CARLYLE is said to have taken Emerson once on a harrowing trip through the London slums and then exclaimed: "Well, do you believe in a devil now?" To Carlyle, Emerson's confident cheerfulness about the world was a curious spectacle; and his wife, Jane, was frankly put off by it. Charles Eliot Norton, son of Andrews who became a friend of Emerson, was similarly perplexed; he regarded Emerson's optimism as a kind of bigotry and said that if Emerson went to hell by mistake he would probably either deny its existence or pronounce it the abode of good and the realm of order. "He has not allowed himself to doubt the supremacy of the best in the moral order," wrote Norton impatiently. "He is never weary of declaring the superiority of assertion and faith over negation!"

Norton's was a common complaint in Emerson's own day and after. Hawthorne, whose dark novels repelled Emerson, called Emerson a "mystic, stretching his hand out of cloudland, in vain search for something real," and he satirized Transcendentalism in his story "The Celestial Railroad." Herman Melville also had satirical things to say about Transcendentalism in *The Confidence Man*; and in both *Moby Dick* (1851) and *Pierre* (1852) he took sharp issue with some of its basic affirmations. John Morley rebuked Emerson for overlooking "the vileness, the cruelty, the utter despicableness to which humanity may be moulded"; Henry James, Jr., thought Emerson's "ripe unconsciousness of evil" gave him a narrowly limited view of the world; George Santayana said that Emersonian Transcendentalism ignored injustice, suffering, and impotence in the world; and William Butler Yeats regarded it as superficial because it lacked a vision of evil. "I love your *Dial*," Carlyle once told Emerson,

> and yet it is with a kind of shudder. You seem to be in danger of dividing yourself from the Fact of this present universe, in which alone, ugly as it is, can I find any anchorage, and soaring away after Ideas, Beliefs, Revelations, and suchlike—into perilous altitudes, as I think. . . . Alas, it is so easy to screw one's self up into high and ever higher altitudes of Transcendentalism, and see nothing under one but the everlasting snows of Himmalayeh ... easy ... but where does it lead? Well, I do believe, for one thing, a man has no right to say to his own generation, turning quite away from it: "Be damned!" It is the whole Past and the whole Future, this same cotton-spinning, dollar-hunting, canting and shrieking, very wretched generation of ours. Come back into it, I tell you.

Edgar Allan Poe, for his part, said he would like to hang the editor of *The Dial*.

Charges of Transcendental insensitivity to the dark side of life could be multiplied almost indefinitely, but they all tended to be overstated. The Transcendentalists were not precisely complacent optimists; they found much to rail against in their own day and age. Emerson has been called a "militant Pollyanna," yet he was not unaware of the sadness of things. He once referred to the "ghastly reality of things" and decided, when he was thirty-two, that after the age of thirty a person wakes up sad most mornings the rest of his life. There was an austere—even bleak—note in Transcendentalism, for all its joyous assertions; and Europeans like Nietzsche, Baudelaire, and Gide, scarcely noted for their facile optimism, read Emerson's essays with profound respect and admiration. Still, there is no doubt that the Transcendentalists regarded their faith as an invigorating one and that they preferred (especially in the salad days of the movement) affirmation to negation. When Emerson and Margaret Fuller got out the first number of *The Dial* in July, 1840, they announced in a letter from the editors to the readers, their clear intention of elevating people to a higher platform of aspiration, making life less desultory, and removing melancholy from the landscape. "We wish," they said, explaining the name *Dial*, "it may resemble that instrument in its celebrated happiness, that of measuring no hours but those of sunshine. Let it be one cheerful rational voice amidst the din of mourners and polemics." During its four years of existence, *The Dial* succeeded in faithfully (too faithfully, Carlyle thought) recording the sunshine. In addition to publishing poetry, literary criticism, book reviews, and discussions of music, painting, sculpture, and religion, it also presented such essays as "The Divine Presence in Nature and the Soul," "The Art of Life," "Ideals of Everyday Life," "What Is Beauty?" and "Christ's Idea of Society." In its last issue, April, 1844, Emerson's essay "The Tragic" showed how intellect and moral sense could "ravish us into a region" where "clouds of sorrow cannot arise." And the last sentence in the final number, concluding a short notice of a book on human nature, announced that *"the highest good for man consists in a conscious increase and progression in Being, or assimilation to God."*

Transcendental Hopes

All the Transcendentalists, even the prickly Thoreau, believed deeply in an inevitable *"increase and progression of Being."* "Surely joy is the condition of life," wrote Thoreau in *The Dial*. "I love to live," he wrote elsewhere.

> I love reform better than its modes. There is no history of how bad became better. I believe something, and there is nothing else but that. I know that I am. I know that another is who knows more than I, who takes an interest in me, whose creature, and yet whose kindred, in one sense, am I. I know that the enterprise is worthy. I know that things work well. I have heard no bad news.

As he grew older, Thoreau did become increasingly aware of evil in nature, in the form of decay and death, and at times it gave him pause; to the end, however, he continued to assert "the glory of the universe" and its "steady onward progress." His friend Alcott was even more affirmative about life; his was probably the serenest of all the Transcendental temperaments. "His attitude," said Thoreau admiringly, "is one of greater faith and expectation than that of any man I know." For Alcott, evil was no problem; he minimized its reality. "Evil no *nature* hath," ran one of his imperturbable *Orphic Sayings*; "the loss of good is that which gives Sin its livelihood." What is the bad, he once asked, "but lapse from the good,—the good blindfolded?" He also transcendentalized evil by saying that it was a kind of condiment which gave relish to good or was like the dark background in a picture which made beauty and goodness stand out all the more vividly by its contrast. Parker wrestled with the problem of evil more earnestly than Alcott, but he also concluded that there was more gladness than sadness in the world and that evil was a transient phenomenon in God's creation. Pain and suffering, he said, served as warnings and deterrents to save man from worse mishaps; they also usually came from ignorance and failure of adaptation and were thus indispensable stimuli to efforts to increase our knowledge and understanding of the universe. All in all, then, there was "a perfect system of optimism in the world" for Parker; evil was resolved in a higher good, and there was endless progress toward perfection going on in the universe. Margaret Fuller, for her part, fully shared her friends' optimism. "Evil," she said, echoing Alcott, "is abstraction; Good is accomplishment." She knew frustration and disappointment in abundance, yet she never gave up her faith in "the divine soul of this visible creation, which cannot err or will not sleep, which cannot permit evil to be permanent or its aim of beauty to be eventually frustrated in the smallest particular." She once reduced her creed to two articles of belief: "I believe in Eternal Progression. I believe in a God, a Beauty and Perfection to which I am to strive all my life for assimilation."

If the Transcendentalists believed in the preponderance of good in the universe, they also had high hopes for the future of humanity. "The work of the ages goes on," affirmed Ripley, even after the failure of Brook Farm;

man advances nearer to the freedom which is his birthright; the temporary evils, that are incidental to all transitions from an old order of things to a better, pass away, and are forgotten; the self-sustaining, self-recovering power of liberty, insures the health of the social body; and . . . the serene spirit of humanity unfolds new strength and beauty in the elastic atmosphere of liberty, until its presence is acknowledged universally as benign.

As a social activist, Brownson, like Ripley, thought that humanity had made tremendous progress in past ages and was destined to move steadily forward. "We must neither feel nor act as if all progress was ended," he wrote, "and mankind had attained all the perfection of which he is capable. There is to be a progress through all the future, as there has been one through all the past; but the future progress must always be elaborated in the present." Hedge was another Transcendentalist who believed that society was always moving onward. "Notwithstanding the perpetual flux and reflux which appears on the surface of things," he explained in the article "Progress of Society" (1834), "there has been an undercurrent of improvement coextensive with the whole course of time. There never was an age in which some element of humanity was not making progress." William H. Channing also believed that the end of existence was growth and that progress was the vital law of humanity. He proclaimed his faith in a manifesto appearing in the *Western Messenger* when he took over as editor in May, 1840:

Man's restlessness is a sign of his grand destiny. Even misdirected energies reveal his greatness. The whole discipline of providence is a proof of God's interest and regard. . . . God is training man to the art of virtue. . . . [We] see a progress in the past history of our race; we feel that a mighty power of good is stirring now in society; we believe in the coming of the kingdom of God.

* * *

For J. F. Clarke, the progress of the human race was fixed "by laws as immutable as the nature of God."

Emerson and the Doctrine of Compensation

Of all the Transcendentalists, it was Emerson who pondered the question of evil most deeply and attempted to deal with it most systematically. Yet at times he gave the impression of wanting to evade it, and for that reason he won the reputation of being the "Orpheus of Optimism." He refused to read *Les Misérables*; "I do not read the sad in literature," he explained (with some exaggeration). "Ghastly, ghastly!" he said of *The Scarlet Letter*. "No one ought to write as Hawthorne has." Melancholy, he once said, "is unendurable; grief is abnormal." Pain and sorrow, he told Charles Eliot Norton, are of no account as compared with the joy of living. The only thing grief taught him, he wrote in "Experience" (1840), "is to know how shallow it is. . . . In the death of my son, now more than two years ago, I seem to have lost a beautiful estate—no more. I cannot get it nearer to me." In *Conduct of Life*, he beseeched people with headaches, sciatica, or even thunderstroke not to upset the household with their complaints, at least not in the morning. "Come out of the azure," he begged. "Love the day." In "Spiritual Laws" (1840), he expressed vexation with excessive preoccupation with the problem of evil. "Our young people," he grumbled,

> are diseased with the theological problems of original sin, origin of evil, predestination and the like. These never presented a practical difficulty to any man,—never darkened across any man's road who did not go out of his way to seek them. These are the soul's mumps and measles and whooping-coughs, and those who have not caught them cannot describe their health or prescribe the cure. A simple mind will not know these enemies.

But he was probably thinking of himself when he wrote this passage. When he was only eighteen he made a long entry in his journal centering on the problem of reconciling the presence of evil in the world with Providential goodness. He made no effort at that time to minimize its power. "The enslaved, the sick, the disappointed, the poor, the unfortunate, the dying, the surviving, cry out, It is here," he wrote. "Every man points to his dwelling or strikes his breast to say, It is here. An enumeration of some of the most prominent evils in society will illustrate the variety and malignity of this disease." He spent the next three decades trying to account for the variety and malignity of evil in a Transcendental universe.

In "Compensation," one of the three or four best-known (and most controversial) essays appearing in *Essays, First Series* (1840), Emerson made his first systematic effort to explain how evil can coexist with good in a fundamentally beneficent universe. The idea of "compensation" had been maturing in his mind ever since his student days. It was one of the means by which he enabled himself, like Margaret Fuller, to accept the universe after he abandoned the faith of his fathers; and he touched upon it time and again in his sermons and also in his journals, letters, and lectures. "I am trying to learn the ethical truths that always allure me from my cradle till now," he wrote his brother Edward in 1831, "& yet how slowly disclosed! That word *Compensation* is one of the watchwords of my spiritual world,—& time & chance & sorrow & hope do not by their revelations abate my curiosity." Emerson's main objective in his essay, "Compensation," was to prove that the universe is fundamentally just and that life is basically fair. "Justice is not postponed," he asserted. "A perfect equity adjusts its balance in all parts of life. . . . The dice of God are always loaded. The world looks like a multiplication table, or a mathematical equation, which, turn it how you will, balances itself." Justice always triumphed, Emerson contended, because of the "perfect compensation" represented by the universe. But he stretched the meaning of the word "compensation" to cover a variety of ideas, some of them only remotely related to the basic concept of counterbalance. His essay dealt with polarity and retribution as well as compensation and also with the price paid for the possession of special talents. It also presented a Neoplatonic view of good and evil that practically negated his original thesis that the law of compensation ruled all things.

Emerson began his essay by ridiculing the notion that the injustices of this life are rectified in another world. He did not believe in future rewards and punishments after death. The orthodox belief that the wicked may be successful and the good miserable in this world, but that compensation will be made to both parties in the world to come seemed preposterous to him. But having abandoned the traditional Christian view of immortality, he needed to convince himself that justice prevails in the present world if he was to feel at home in it. He had, in other words, to desupernaturalize rewards and punishments just as he had desupernaturalized Christian miracles and revelation. He did so by placing compensation at the very heart of things in this world. The law of compensation, he said, was at work here and now, and it governed animals as well as human beings and inorganic as well as organic life. There was compensation (or polarity) in mechanics: What we gain in power is lost in time, and the converse. There was compensation in climate and soil: A cold climate invigorates and barren soil does not breed fevers, crocodiles, tigers, or scorpions. There was compensation in the animal kingdom: A surplusage given to one part is paid out of a reduction from another part of the same creature, so that compensation balances every gift and every defect. There was, above all, compensation at work in human life. "Every excess causes a defect; every defect an excess. Every sweet hath its sour; every evil its good. . . . For every grain of wit there is a grain of folly. For every thing you have missed, you have gained something else; and for every thing you gain, you lose something." Emerson spent the rest of his essay exploring the implications of this point of view for humanity.

In explaining how compensation worked, Emerson's major point was that everything in life had its price, either in circumstance or character, and that there was an absolute balance of give and take in the world. This was true of simple misbehavior as well as immorality and crime; the miscreant, the sinner, and the criminal never escaped punishment in this world. For misbehavior of any kind (even if it involved neither serious immorality nor criminal action) there was, Emerson thought, an unavoidable punishment. People always suffer if they mistreat other people. "You cannot do wrong without suffering wrong. . . ," declared Emerson. "Treat men as pawns and ninepins and you shall suffer as well as they. If you leave out their hearts, you shall lose your own." Emerson thought that all infractions of love and equity in social relations were speedily punished. "They are punished by Fear. Whilst I stand in simple relations to my fellow-man, I have no displeasure in meeting him. But as soon as there is any departure from simplicity and attempt at halfness, or good for me that is not good for him, my neighbor feels the wrong; he shrinks from me," and "there is hate in him and fear in me." All social abuses, he thought, sooner or later generate fear and hatred among people, which eventually threaten the very survival of the social order. Cruelty on the part of rulers, moreover, invariably turned out to be self-defeating: if government was oppressive, the ruler's life was in danger; if taxes were exorbitant, the revenue would yield nothing; if the criminal code was too sanguinary, juries would not convict. There were, in short, countervailing forces checking bad behavior in this world.

But if improper behavior was always penalized in some fashion, so was immorality. Immoral actions (by which Emerson meant sensual excess or immoderate concern with one's own private advantage) exacted an inevitable toll. "Every faculty which is a receiver of pleasure," said Emerson, "has an equal penalty put on its abuse. It is to answer for its moderation with its life." If we try to gratify our senses at the expense of our character and integrity, or if we "truck and higgle for a private good," we invariably meet disaster. "Pleasure is taken out of pleasant things, profit out of profitable things, power out of strong things, the moment we seek to separate them from the whole." We can no more enjoy a sensual good by itself apart from the moral and social context, Emerson insisted, than we can get an inside that has no outside or a light which has no shadow. The immoralist always suffers pain sooner or later in Emerson's scheme of things.

Crime, finally, like misbehavior and immorality, was always punished in Emerson's idealistic world. There was an inevitable retribution, he thought, for all criminal acts. Even if the criminal was never physically apprehended, he paid a heavy price for his wrongdoing in terms of fear and guilt. "Crime and punishment grow out of one stem," Emerson maintained. "The thief steals from himself. The swindler swindles from himself." The thief and swindler, for one thing, lose the knowledge and virtue they would have gained had they done the honest work required to obtain anything worthwhile in this world. For another, their crimes degrade and destroy them as human beings. If the criminal persists in his vicious ways and isn't brought to judgment, law-abiding citizens naturally feel defrauded of the retribution due to evil acts; but they should remember, Emerson said, that inasmuch as the criminal "carries the malignity and the lie with him he so far decreases from nature," and, even if it is not apparent, "this deadly deduction makes square the eternal account." The writer John Erskine was exasperated by Emerson's reasoning at this point (and so were many other people). "The thief is punished, though the police never find him," he commented dryly, "for the price of theft is loss of innocence, fear of arrest, suspicion of other men. What compensation is destined for the victim of the thief, optimistic Transcendentalism preferred not to investigate." But Emerson did think there were compensations for victims of bad luck in this life. Before taking them up in his essay, however, he was anxious to explore the ramifications of compensation for recipients of good luck.

In Emerson's system, there was not only a penalty for wrongdoing; there was also a price to be paid for exceptional good fortune. "Benefit is the end of nature," said Emerson. "But for every benefit you receive a tax is levied." Emerson was bothered by the natural inequalities appearing among human beings as well as by the wide variance in circumstantial opportunities available to different people, and he felt the need to show that there were compensations for these seeming injustices in a Transcendental universe. "The radical tragedy of nature," he admitted, "seems to be the distinction of More or Less. How can Less not feel the pain; how not feel indignation or malevolence toward the More?" It was hard not to feel that there was something unjust about the unequal distribution of talents in the world. But Emerson thought it was possible to demonstrate the workings of the law of compensation here as elsewhere. One way to equalize things was to point out that there was a price exacted for all good fortune; and another way was to show that there were compensations for apparent bad luck. In demonstrating the former, however, Emerson got himself into a dilemma from which he was able to extract himself only by transcending the whole elaborate scheme of compensations which he had taken such pains to erect.

Emerson believed that varieties of condition tended to equalize themselves; nature always kept a balance. "There is always some levelling circumstance that puts down the overbearing, the strong, the rich, the fortunate, substantially on the same ground with all others." The President of the United States, for example, paid dearly in peace of mind for his exalted position; so did other recipients of fame, power, and fortune. With exceptional ability always came extraordinary responsibility. "He who by force of will or of thought is great and overlooks thousands, has the responsibility of overlooking. With every influx of light come new dangers." Talented people must pay a price for their native gifts in terms of severe discipline and hard work; if they do not, their talents go to waste and they experience failure and defeat. A literary, musical, or artistic genius has to give up many things enjoyed by ordinary people in order to develop his creative gifts; he may have to neglect family and friends and even alienate himself from the world so that he can focus all his attention on the creative impulse, which is both gift and obligation. It is foolish to envy people born with greater talents than we possess. Great talent exacts a heavy price; and if one is unwilling (and most people are) to pay the price of disciplined effort that develops natural talent, it will all come to naught. "Thus do all things preach the indifferency of circumstances," said Emerson. We should do the best we can with what we have got and not rail at fortune. "The man is all. Every thing has two sides, a good and an evil. Every advantage has its tax. I learn to be content."

Still, if every advantage had its drawbacks and every

good its evil, what incentive was there for conscientious behavior? Was it not a fact that on Emerson's reasoning there was little point in striving to do well? If good and evil were so inextricably related that whenever we gained any good we had to pay heavily for it and whenever we lost one good we gained another, were not all actions indifferent? Emerson admitted the force of this objection to his doctrine, and at this point he abandoned compensation for a Plotinian view of good and evil. "There is a deeper fact in the soul than compensation," he declared,

> to wit, its own nature. The soul is not a compensation, but life. The soul *is*. Under all this running sea of circumstance, whose waters ebb and flow with perfect balance, lies the aboriginal abyss of Being. Existence, or God, is not a relation or a part, but the whole. Being is the vast affirmative, excluding negation, self-balanced and swallowing up all relations, parts and times within itself. Nature, truth, virtue, are the influx from thence. Vice is the absence or departure of the same. Nothing, falsehood, may indeed stand as the great Night or shade on which as a background the living universe paints itself forth; but no fact is begotten by it; it cannot work, for it is not. It cannot work any good; it cannot work any harm. It is harm inasmuch as it is worse not to be than to be.

Emerson, in other words, resorted to the Neoplatonic definition of evil as nonbeing or absence of being in order to save his system. (This was not new with him. In his Divinity School Address he had told the Harvard students that good was positive and evil merely privative, like cold, which was the privation of heat: "All evil is so much death or nonentity. Benevolence is absolute and real.") But if good was pure being and evil absence of being, it followed that there was no penalty attached to the achievement of virtue and wisdom, for they involved an increase of good in the world. Merely *external* goods (like property, for example) indeed had their price; and if we obtained them without our own efforts they had no roots in us and gave us no advantage. But virtue and wisdom were *internal* goods which we could achieve only by ourselves and they carried no price, tax, penalty, or toll. The gain of rectitude brought no loss with it; nor did the achievement of knowledge (for example, knowledge of the law of compensation) hurt us. "There is no penalty to virtue; no penalty to wisdom," said Emerson;

> they are proper additions of being. In a virtuous action I properly *am*; in a virtuous act I add to the world; I plant into deserts conquered from Chaos and Nothing and see the darkness receding on the limits of the horizon. There can be no excess to love, none to knowledge, none to beauty, when these attributes are considered in the purest sense. The soul refuses all limits. It affirms in man always an Optimism, never a Pessimism.

But it was precisely in the development of mind and spirit toward ever-greater wisdom and virtue that Emerson found a compensation for inequalities of condition. If one realizes his affinity with other human beings, as a wise person does, then the "bitterness of *His* and *Mine* ceases." By loving his fellow men, he learns from them and thus enriches his own life. Instead of envying talented people for their superior natural-born gifts, we can accept their achievements as a marvelous enrichment of our own lives and thus incorporate the fruits of their genius into ourselves. By our love of great art we share in the artist's accomplishments. We can make

Shakespeare our very own; Beethoven can become one with us. And if we are wise, we will see that there are compensations for calamities as well as for inequalities of condition. The experience of failure, frustration, and disappointment can be educative; what seems intolerable to us at first may turn out in the long run to contribute mightily to our moral and spiritual growth. The final proof of the ceaseless operation of the law of compensation, Emerson thought, lay in the part which calamity plays in the development of character:

> A fever, a mutilation, a cruel disappointment, a loss of wealth, a loss of friends, seems at the moment unpaid loss, and unpayable. But the sure years reveal the deep remedial force that underlies all facts. The death of a dear friend, wife, brother, lover, which seemed nothing but privation, somewhat later assumes the aspect of a guide or genius; for it commonly operates revolutions in our way of life, terminates an epoch of infancy or of youth which was waiting to be closed, breaks up a wonted occupation, or a household, or style of living, and allows the formation of new ones more friendly to the growth of character. . . .

To later generations of Americans Emerson's law of compensation has been the least acceptable of all Transcendental doctrines. Critics have condemned it as shallow, unconvincing, even absurd. Emerson has been chided for ignoring the hard facts of life, for refusing to recognize that we sometimes receive evil for evil as well as good for evil, and for elevating justice above pity, mercy, and love. He also overlooked the social background of moral incentives; in a hedonistic society remorse and guilt could hardly play the part which the Puritan Emerson assigned them in his great drama of psychological retribution. And yet, despite Emerson's tendency to overstate his thesis, to subsume too many particulars under his general principles, and to neglect the part that chance plays in the universe, there was undeniable truth in much of what he said and his essay continues to evoke interest. Limitations may be converted into opportunities (though in certain respects they remain limitations for all that); calamities may be educative (though they may also be too destructive to be ennobling). In a universe characterized by death and decay as well as by life and growth, there is surely much force in Emerson's contention that our final dependence must be on inner resources rather than on the contingencies of circumstance. He was also probably right in regarding life itself as an optimism and the availing oneself of the great gifts of life as a tremendous affirmation. And yet it is difficult to read without astonishment his confession of faith to a friend, in a letter of July 3, 1841: "My creed is very simple, that Goodness is the only Reality, that to Goodness alone can we trust, to that we may trust all & always; beautiful and blessed and blessing is it, though it should seem to slay." There is no blinking the fact: Emerson was essentially a happy man. He loved his country, his town, his wife and his family, enjoyed his friends and associates, was exhilarated by natural beauty, and thrived in his vocation as scholar, lecturer, and moral essayist. He experienced serious illness as a youth and he suffered several tragic losses in his family, and yet he counted himself fortunate on the whole and rejoiced in his life. His temperament was serene and cheerful, and most of his days were happy ones. He once wrote that he compared notes with a friend who "expects everything of the universe and is disappointed when anything is less than the best, and I found that I begin at the other extreme, expecting nothing, and am always full of thanks for moderate goods. . . . If we take the good we find, asking no questions, we shall have heaping measures." When a millennialist tried to rouse his fears about the imminent end of the world, he brushed him aside impatiently: "Well, let it go; we can get on just as well without it." "When you looked at Emerson," Walt Whitman observed, "it never occurred to you that there could be any villainies in the world." "It is now imputed as a shortcoming," commented Emerson's son Edward, "that he did not do justice to the prevailing power of evil in the world. Fortunately he did not. It was not the message given to him. He could not. For that which made him live and serve and love and be loved was—a good Hope."

Emerson nourished a good hope to the end of his days. His Transcendentalism was essentially a philosophy of good hope, which looked to the future instead of to the past and which saw possibilities rather than limitations. Above all, Emerson's philosophy emphasized strength of character. Emerson thought it was weak and cowardly to whine about one's ill fortune. A good Transcendentalist should steel himself to face adversity with dignity and courage and seek ever to transmute obstacles into opportunities. Emerson would have enjoyed Ernest Hemingway's remark that whatever happens to a man is his own damned fault if he is any good at all. He wanted people to devise their own compensations for whatever unpleasantness they encountered. Compensation for Emerson was fundamentally a creative act by which a person asserted his mastery over circumstances and bent them to his own will. Yet despite the air of certainty with which he discussed these things, Emerson was not entirely sure that he had really settled the problem of adversity once for all; nor was he completely satisfied with the disposition he had made of evil in his compensatory scheme. He came more and more to believe that no theory of life was convincing that did not give prominence to vice, pain, disease, poverty, insecurity, disunion, fear, and death. In his essay for *The Dial* in April, 1844, "The Tragic," Emerson, it is true, continued to assert that sorrow dwelt in a low region, that tragedy lay in the eye of the beholder, and that intellect and moral sense could always find ethical and aesthetic compensations for bad fortune. Nevertheless, he gave greater recognition to the "tragic element" than he had ever done before. "He has seen but half the universe who never has been shown the house of Pain," he declared. "As the salt sea covers more than two thirds of the surface of the globe, so sorrow encroaches in man on felicity."

The Power of Fate

During the 1840's, Emerson's philosophy took on a more somber tone. Emerson did not exactly repudiate his earlier faith in individual possibilities; but he began quietly shifting his attention to the power of circumstances to hem people in and frustrate their wishes. "The word Fate, or Destiny," he said in a lecture on Michel de Montaigne in 1845,

expresses the sense of mankind, in all ages, that the laws of the world do not always befriend us, but often hurt and crush us. . . . We have too little power of resistance against this ferocity which champs us up. What front can we make against these unavoidable, victorious, maleficent forces? What can I do against the influence of Race, in my history? What can I do against hereditary and constitutional habits; against scrofula, lymph, impotence? against climate, against barbarism in my country? I can reason down or deny everything, except this perpetual Belly: feed he must and will, and I cannot make him respectable.

* * *

Yet Emerson emphatically rejected the notion that "pure malignity" formed any part of the universe. To believe in the independent power of evil was, he thought, pure and simple atheism; it was the "last profanation." He rejected, too, the fatalistic view of life appearing in Greek tragedy, East Indian mythology, and Turkish predestination. To say that brute Fate or Destiny controlled the order of nature and events (serving man if his wishes happened to lie in the same course, crushing him if his wishes lay contrary to it, and forever heedless of whether it served or crushed him) was to say that "an immense whim" governed things. Emerson ranked belief in implacable Destiny with popular superstitions about spilling salt, knocking on wood, and reciting the Lord's Prayer backwards. It not only deteleologized creation; it also derationalized man. Circumstances were indeed powerful; but so was human intellect. It was important, Emerson thought, to distinguish superstitious fatalism from the doctrine of philosophical necessity, which asserted a meaningful connection between things and events which it was possible for human beings to discern and utilize for beneficial purposes. Yet, having dismissed brute Fate as the ultimate irrationality, Emerson acknowledged that our private wishes were frequently frustrated by the laws of the world. "The law which establishes nature and the human race," he said, "continually thwarts the will of ignorant individuals, and this in the particulars of disease, want, insecurity, and disunion." It was the will of "*ignorant* individuals," however, that was thwarted; Emerson never lost his faith in an increase of knowledge and a diminution of ignorance as a means of surmounting the difficulties of life and coping with fate.

The most brilliant essay of Emerson's later period was devoted entirely to the subject of fate. Presented as a lecture in the early 1850's and rewritten for publication, "Fate" came first in the book of essays entitled *The Con-*

duct of Life, appearing in 1860. In "Fate," Emerson grappled with the problem of evil anew; he also attempted to strike a balance between freedom and fate, the individual and the world, and between intellect and nature. There were no longer any qualifications in his portrayal of the darker and harsher elements forming part of human existence. "I dip my pen in the blackest ink," he told friends, "because I am not afraid of falling into my ink-pot." In "Fate," Emerson charged Americans with superficiality; they did not face the "terrors of life" honestly and courageously, as all great men and nations have done. Nature was no sentimentalist, Emerson assured his countrymen; the world was rough and surly and it did not mind drowning people, freezing them to death, overwhelming them with storms, floods, earthquakes, and volcanic eruptions, and striking them down with scurvy, cholera, smallpox, and other diseases. "The way of Providence is a little rude." Heredity, moreover, could be just as cruel and ruthless as environment. "How shall a man escape from his ancestor," exclaimed Emerson, "or draw off from his veins the black drop which he drew from his father's or his mother's life?"

> Men are what their mothers made them. . . . When each comes forth from his mother's womb, the gate of gifts closes behind him. Let him value his hand and feet, he has but one pair. So he has but one future, and that is already predetermined in his lobes. . . . All the privilege and all the legislation of the world cannot meddle or help to make a poet or a prince out of him.

Life, moreover, preyed on life; no less than snakes, spiders, and tigers were human beings involved in the general slaughter by which living creatures procure sustenance, even though they tried daintily to conceal it at the dinner table. The new science of statistics, Emerson noted, confirmed the fact that life can be hard and cruel; it revealed that famine, typhus, frost, war, and suicide were calculable parts of human existence. "The force with which we resist these torrents of tendency" looked ridiculously inadequate to Emerson. "Let us not deny it up and down," he cried. "Providence has a wild, rough, incalculable road to its end, and it is of no use to try to whitewash its huge, unmixed instrumentalities, or to dress up that terrific benefactor in a clean shirt and white neckcloth of a student in divinity."

Still, Providence remained a "benefactor" for Emerson; "terrific," indeed, but a benefactor nonetheless. Fate was powerful, Emerson conceded, but, properly conceived, it could be surmounted and rendered harmless, even advantageous. Emerson defined Fate as the laws of the world; they operated with "irresistible dictation" on human beings and placed impassable limits on what humans might do. Imperfectly grasped, these laws hemmed people in on every side and buffeted them about mercilessly. Correctly understood, though, they could be utilized for human purposes. By using his mind, man could become a "stupendous antagonism" to Fate; with knowledge and insight, he could become "a piece of causation" himself and counteract the power of Fate. "So far as a man thinks," said Emerson, "he is free." ("You conquer Fate," averred Thoreau, "by thought.") From the intellectual point of view, Fate was a name for facts not yet passed under the fire of thought and for causes still unpenetrated. But every solid in the universe became fluid on the approach of mind; every "jet of chaos which threatens to exterminate us is convertible by intellect into a wholesome force." The water drowns ship and sailor like a grain of dust; learn to swim and trim your bark and the wave becomes a plume and a power. The cold freezes man like a dewdrop; learn to skate and the ice gives you a graceful motion. Right drainage destroys typhus; lemon juice heals scurvy; vaccination ends smallpox; science transforms steam from a mystery into a powerful servant of man. The lessons of Fate were no longer odious when one realized that comprehension of natural processes could make weapons and wings of what appeared to be hostile forces. Calamities could be stimuli to insight and spurs to action; they could assist humanity in its steady advance out of Fate into freedom. "If Fate is ore and quarry," said Emerson, "if evil is good in the making, if limitation is power that shall be, if calamities, oppositions, and weights are wings and means,—we are reconciled." The universe was from this point of view dual in nature: mental and physical. "History," Emerson decided, "is the action and reaction of these two,—Nature and Thought; two boys pushing each other on the curbstone of the pavement. Everything is pusher or pushed; and matter and mind are in perpetual tilt and balance, so."

The Double Consciousness

But even after transcendentalizing Fate into freedom, Emerson did not deny that it operated with implacable cruelty on the lives of particular individuals. Still, this was the way it should be, he decided. A child who knows no better puts his hand into the fire and is badly burned; we grieve over the burning, but, Emerson pointed out, it would be foolish for us to wish that fire did not burn. The burnt hand is deplorable; the fact that fire always burns is one of the glories of the universe. Disease carries off thousands of persons until, from their fate, we learn how to stave it off or cure it and thus benefit the rest of the race. Heredity is frequently cruel; but if we learn its laws we will be glad they work as they do, for perhaps we can turn them to humanity's benefit. Emerson thought we must learn to rise above particulars into universals; we must come to realize that the universe is a complex of majestic natural laws which operate ruthlessly when infringed but which serve mankind marvelously when comprehended and assented to. When disaster strikes, he advised, we should not curse the world; we should remember that disaster is preferable to a suspension of the laws of nature. "If in the least particular one could derange the order of nature," he said, "—who would accept the gift of life?" Not Emerson surely. And not Parker either. Like Emerson, Parker thought it was absurd for people to want God to "twist the material world" to accommodate human folly or to alter natural processes from moment to moment to suit the caprices of human beings. Emerson proposed what he called "double consciousness" as the final solution to the problem of evil: consciousness of public as well as of private good. "A man," he said,

> must ride alternately on the horses of his private and his public nature. . . . So when a man is the victim of his fate, has sciatica in his loins and cramp in his mind; a club-foot and a club in his wit; a sour face and a selfish temper; a strut in his gait and a conceit in his affection; or is ground to powder by the vice of his race;—he is to rally on his relation to the Universe, which his ruin benefits. Leaving the daemon [personal spirit] who suffers, he is to take sides with the Deity who secures universal benefit by his pain.

The final compensation for evil, then, lay in recognizing that although natural law may work to the detriment of the individual, it always operates for the good of the whole. Emerson ended his essay "Fate" with a paean to the Blessed Unity and Beautiful Necessity which he saw pervading the world and to the divine law which "vivifies nature" and "solicits the pure in heart to draw on all its omnipotence."

The swamping of the individual in the universe was not entirely new for Emerson. Transcendentalism, from the start, had rested on a precarious balance between individualism and universalism. The Transcendentalists had at the outset urged individuals to act boldly, independently, and creatively, but at the same time they had located the source for individual vitality in Universal Spirit. Even when Emerson was preaching a heady kind of individualism in the early years of Transcendentalism, he was also asserting calmly that "the individual is always mistaken." In "Experience" (1841), he declared that "nothing is of us or our works"; everything, he explained, "is of God. . . . All writing comes by grace of God, and all doing and having." He had tried for a time, it is true, to find individual compensations for natural and moral evil, and he had come close to thinking that handicaps could always be converted into assets. But at length he abandoned the quest for perfect justice for the individual as futile; the consolation for individual suffering, he decided, rested finally on a Transcendental faith in the goodness of creation at large. He never doubted that for all its "odious facts," the universe was "the work of a great and beneficient progressive necessity." He acknowledged, however, that the "sublime and friendly Destiny" guiding the human race seemed harsh and cruel at times:

It may be styled a cruel kindness, serving the whole even to the ruin of the member; a terrible communist, reserving all profits to the community, without dividend to individuals. Its law is, you shall have everything as a member, nothing to yourself. For Nature is the noblest engineer, yet uses a grinding economy, working up all that is wasted today

into tomorrow's creation;—not a superfluous grain
of sand, for all the ostentation she makes of expense
and public works. It is because Nature thus saves
and uses, laboring for the general, that we poor
particulars are so crushed and straitened, and find it
so hard to live.

But each generation forms part of the splendor and
grace of the universe and contributes to the general
advance. The central intention of the universe was love,
good, beauty, harmony, and joy, Emerson insisted, and
there was perpetual melioration at work in both nature
and humanity. Transcendentalism's indispensable tenet
was faith in the beneficent tendency of the universe.

Emerson and Melville

In 1849, Herman Melville heard Emerson lecture in
Boston; he was impressed by the brilliance and nobility
of "this Plato who talks thro' his nose," but had serious
reservations about his general outlook. "I could readily
see in Emerson, notwithstanding his merit, a gaping
flaw," Melville told a friend. "It was the insinuation, that
had he lived in those days when the world was made, he
might have offered some valuable suggestions." Melville
misread Emerson in this regard. For Emerson had no
suggestions to make; he was pleased with what he believed the universe's central purposes to be and quite
satisfied with its general operations. But Melville was
right in sensing a fundamental difference between his
outlook and Emerson's. Reading Emerson's essays later
on, he continued to be impressed with Emerson's high-
mindedness and with his penetrating insights, but he was
put off by Emerson's feeling that he had somehow
fathomed the mystery of existence. Unlike Emerson,
Melville was filled with doubts. He wondered whether

the question What is Truth? was "more final than any answer." But Emerson, in a poem called "The Sphinx" (1841), his favorite, has a poet penetrate the sphinx's riddle: despite the multifarious appearances which the divine energy takes, there is a basic unity joining all particulars in the world together, making man at one with nature. In the chapter "The Sphynx" in *Moby Dick*, Melville, by contrast, leaves the riddle forever unsolved. He has Captain Ahab address the head of a sperm whale as if it were the sphinx: "Of all divers, thou hast dived the deepest. . . . O head! thou hast seen enough to split the planets and make an infidel of Abraham, and not one syllable is thine!" But Emerson did not deny that creation poses endless riddles; he simply had a greater faith than Melville in man's capacity to cope with them. "Undoubtedly," he said, "we have no questions which are unanswerable. We must trust the perfection of the creation so far as to believe that whatever curiosity the order of things has awakened in our minds the order of things can satisfy." Emerson once dreamed that he was floating freely through the air and came upon the world shrunken to the size of an apple. "Then," he recalled, "an angel took it in his hand and brought it to me and said, 'This must thou eat.' And I ate the world." And the world was very much to his taste; he was firm in his belief that a beneficent tendency was at work amid the flux of things. It was all quite different with Melville. In his world, "mysteries ever open into mysteries," and one was afloat on uncharted seas. "Why, ever since Adam," he exclaimed to Hawthorne, "who has got to the meaning of this great allegory, the world?"

Emerson's serene tranquillity and imperturbable calm deeply offended Melville. Emerson, he thought, was always jumping into the pulpit in his essays; he "still bethinks himself of his optimism—he must make that good somehow against the eternal hell itself." Melville thought that a person who "hath more of joy than sorrow in him" was "not true, or undeveloped." His Ahab did not accept the universe; he saw an implacable evil and an inscrutable malice at its heart, and he raved and ranted at it and vented all the hatred and wrath he could summon against it. "Toward thee I roll," he raged, "thou all-destroying but unconquering whole; to the last I grapple with thee; from hell's heart I stab at thee; for hate's sake I spit my last breath at thee." The fate that Emerson domesticated by identifying it with beneficent tendency, Melville saw, in *Moby Dick*, as blind, senseless, capricious, malignant, and irresistible power. And yet Melville could not help admiring Emerson. For the sake of argument, he said to Evert Duyckinck, let us call Emerson a fool. "Then had I rather be a fool than a wise man.—I love all men who *dive*. Any fish can swim near the surface, but it takes a great whale to go down stairs five miles or more. . . ."

Emerson, for his part, did not dismiss skeptics like Melville with impatience or disdain; the skeptical Montaigne was one of his favorite writers. For all his affirmations, he experienced doubt himself on occasion. Throughout nature, he once observed, there is "something mocking, something that leads us on and on, but arrives nowhere; keeps no faith with us." Nature, he decided, "resents generalizing, and insults the Philosopher in every moment with a million fresh particulars. . . ." He admitted that while he was in his study his faith was perfect, but that it "breaks, scatters, becomes compounded in converse with men." Yet despite occasional skeptical moods Emerson regarded himself as basically a believer. "Men seem to be constitutionally believers and unbelievers," he mused.

There is no bridge that can cross from a mind in one state to a mind in the other. All my opinions, affections, whimsies, are tinged with belief,—all incline to that side. . . . But I cannot give reasons to a person of different persuasion that are at all adequate to the force of my conviction. Yet when I fail to find the reason, my faith is not less.

In their teleological view of creation, Transcendentalists like Emerson were profoundly optimistic. Their vision may have been austere, but it was hopeful, not tragic, in the large. Like Hegel (and like Marx, too), they believed in cosmic progress; they thought the world was unfolding according to an immanent, necessary, and beneficent plan. It is a view which still has a powerful appeal for many people and nations in the contemporary world.

CHAPTER SIX

Transience and Permanence

IN his South Boston sermon "The Transient and Permanent in Christianity" in May, 1841, Theodore Parker separated what he regarded as the intrinsic truths of the Christian religion from its ephemeral forms, rites, and creeds, identified the former with Transcendentalism, and pronounced them to be of enduring value for men and women everywhere. Yet there were undoubted parochial elements in Parker's own Transcendentalism. Emerson himself acknowledged that no one could "quite emancipate himself from his age and country, or produce a model in which the education, the religion, the politics, usages and arts of his times shall have no share. Though he were never so original, never so wilful and fantastic, he cannot wipe out of his work every trace of the thoughts amidst which it grew." A century after the heyday of the Newness some observers regarded Transcendentalism as little more than a quaint anachronism. "Concord in 1840 was an idyllic moment in the history of the race," declared historian James T. Adams in 1930. "That moment came and passed, like a baby's smile." Yet the Transcendentalists—especially Emerson and Thoreau—have never ceased to engage the interest of later generations of Americans, and there are important respects in which they speak directly, even insistently, to our own age. There were unquestionably transcendent as well as transient elements in the New Views, as there were in the Christianity that Parker was criticizing.

Criticism by Contemporaries

One sign of transcendence was the outrage that the New Views aroused among contemporaries. Representatives of the established order thought the Transcendentalists were horrendously innovative, and, as is usual in such cases, they accused them of being vague, abstruse, impractical, unintelligible, paradoxical, enigmatic, and misleading for young people. One critic coined the ugliest synonym he could think of for Transcendentalism: *"Incomprehensibilityosityivityalityationmentnessism."* Even Hawthorne, a close associate of the Concord group, thought there might be something in the charge of obscurity. In "The Celestial Railroad," he described a Transcendentalist as follows:

> He is a German by birth, and is called Giant Transcendentalist; but as to his form, his features, his substance, and his nature generally, it is the chief peculiarity of this huge miscreant that neither he for himself, nor anybody for him, has ever been able to describe them.... He shouted at us, but in so strange a phraseology that we knew not what he meant, nor whether to be encouraged or affrighted.

Transcendentalism unquestionably had its excesses: Jones Very transcribing messages from the Holy Ghost; Charles Lane trying to break up Alcott's home in the name of communal idealism; the Fruitlander who ate only crackers one year and only apples the next; his associate who stayed home naked all day because he thought clothes unspiritual; young Ellery Channing proclaiming, "I am universal; I have nothing to do with the particular and definite"; and the ill-kempt young Emersonidae who came to Emerson's house without shoes to shout and harangue and indulge their coprolalia. Bronson Alcott's utterances were occasionally ineffable ("He omnipresent is, All round himself he lies"), and even phrases in Emerson, lifted out of context, could sound silly. Christopher Cranch and James Clarke had fun doing caricatures of such Emersonian lines as "I expand like corn and melons," and "I become a transparent eyeball," but Emerson, who was not often excessively solemn, enjoyed the sketches. And he also insisted, defiantly, that the Transcendentalists had their feet firmly on the ground. In "The Conservative" (1841), he even warned reformers against attempting too much. "For the existing world is not a dream," he reminded them,

> and cannot with impunity be treated as a dream; neither is it a disease; but it is the ground on which you stand, it is the mother of whom you were born. Reform converses with possibilities, perchance with impossibilities, but here is sacred fact. This also was true, or it could not be: it had life in it, or it could not have existed; it has life in it, or it could not continue.

Yet it was also a fact that the Transcendentalists encouraged freethinking in religion and critical reflection in all fields. Their opponents may have called them misty and obscure, but they understood perfectly the Transcendental threat to traditional ways of looking at things.

The Transcendental emphasis on intuition provoked a second criticism: that proponents of the Newness were contemptuous of history, indifferent to customs and institutions, oblivious to social experience, and friendly to anarchy and antinomianism. There was some truth in the charge, as the Transcendentalists cheerfully admitted; insofar as they appealed to a higher law, "out of time, out of space, and not subject to circumstance," they were indeed attempting to emancipate the individual from history in his moral behavior. The Transcendentalists' excoriation of the Christian church and their contempt for the political state, strictures on the business community, and militant abolitionism in the 1850's were all founded on the conviction that political and social institutions should be judged by spiritual laws transcending time and place, not by utilitarian criteria. Orestes Brownson, after leaving Transcendentalism and turning against it, accused his former associates of abandoning the restraints of reason, giving loose rein to imagination and passion, and encouraging wild dreams and strange fancies that could only destroy civilized behavior. But, in point of fact, he could not have been more mistaken. For all their paeans to instinct and impulse, the Transcendentalists kept close rein on their feelings. "The child, the infant, is a transcendentalist, and charms us all," Emerson once wrote in his journal; "we try to be, and instantly run in debt, lie, steal, commit adultery, go mad, and die." Despite the pronounced note of transhistoricism in many of their utterances, the Transcendentalists, except possibly Alcott, were by no means indifferent to the imperatives of social experience. In "The Conservative," Emerson expressed considerable sympathy for the Burkean point of view. Although the commands of conscience are *essentially* absolute," he declared, they are *historically* limitary." We cannot seek a "literal rectitude," he went on to say, "but an useful, that is, a conditioned one, such a one as the faculties of man and the constitution of things will warrant." He added that there was a natural predisposition in favor of age, ancestors, and tradition and that just as a person could not put a boat out to sea without pushing the shore, so a reformer was under the necessity of "using the Actual order of things, in order to disuse it; to live by it, whilst you wish to take away its life." In the poem "Grace" in *The Dial* of January, 1842, Emerson thanked God for providing example and custom as defenses against sin. Any good Unitarian—or Calvinist—could have said the same.

Transcendentalism and Puritanism

The fact is that the Transcendentalists, despite their religious radicalism and their affinities with European Romantic individualism, were heavily indebted to their Puritan heritage. They were no less Puritan in their general life style than Unitarians like Andrews Norton or Presbyterians like Charles Hodge. The wrathful Deity, original sin, special election, and eternal damnation were gone; but the moral idealism, the asceticism, and the doctrine of calling remained. In Transcendentalism, predestination was transmuted into beneficent necessity and the doctrine of grace into creative inspiration, but the moral fervor remained as strong as ever. To some observers, Transcendentalism seemed like Puritanism with all that was harsh and forbidding about the Puritans removed; to others, Transcendentalism seemed closely allied to Puritanism in its moral rigor and its distrust of the sensual side of human nature. "A Transcendentalist," complained Isaac Hecker, the son of German immigrants, who spent some time at Brook Farm, "is one who has keen sight but little warmth of heart; who has fine conceits, but is destitute of the rich glow of love." Walt Whitman regarded himself as something of a Transcendentalist, and the New Englanders admired his work. But his earthiness put them off, and for his part he never felt quite comfortable with them. Melville grumbled that Emerson's "belly, Sir, is in his chest, and his brains descend down into his neck, and offer an obstacle to a draughtful of ale or a mouthful of cake. . . ." When one critic remarked that "one can learn no more of human nature from Emerson than from an Italian opera," his friend corrected him: "Not so much; from an Italian opera one can at least learn that there are two sexes."

Emerson never denied his Puritan sympathies. "What a debt is ours," he once exclaimed, "to that old religion which in the childhood of most of us, still dwelt like a Sabbath morning in the country of New England, teaching privation, self-denial, and sorrow!" To an older clergyman he expressed nostalgic affection for the unpainted churches, strict platforms, iron-gray deacon, and "wearisome prayer, rich with the diction of age" of the Puritans. Theodore Parker felt somewhat the same. Though he helped organize an anti-Sabbath convention in 1848 to fight penal laws on Sunday, he admitted to a friend that he feared "a reaction from the sour, stiff, Jewish way of keeping Sunday into a low, coarse, material, voluptuous or mere money-making abuse of it." And in a resolution he submitted to the convention he stated that "we should lament to see the Sunday devoted to *labor* or *sport*; for though we think all days are equally holy we yet consider that the custom of devoting one day in each week mainly to spiritual culture is still of great advantage to mankind." Emerson agreed. One Sunday morning when he discovered his children playing cards, he was extremely upset. "No! No! No! Put them away," he cried. "Never affront the sacred morning with the sight of cards. When the day's work is done or you are sick, then perhaps they will do, but never in the daylight! No!" On another Sunday, when it was raining, Mrs. Emerson gave the children permission to play battledore and shuttlecock, but when Emerson heard the noise of the game he interceded at once. "That sound was never heard in New England before on Sunday," he said solemnly, "and must not be in my house. Put them away." Both he and his wife were deeply offended when some zealous Emersonidae visiting them took the line that Jesus and his disciples faked the crucifixion in order to sway the mob. It was odious, Emerson told his wife afterward, "to have lilies pulled up and skunk-cabbages planted in their places." Years later, as a member of the Board of Overseers of Harvard College, he supported compulsory chapel for the students, and it was regarded as a regrettable lapse of old age; it was probably also a relapse into childhood habits. Emerson's religious radicalism was real enough, and American freethinkers were heavily in his debt. But the Puritanism stemming from a long line of clergymen in his family background left a deep imprint on him.

In his attitude toward work as well as in his transcendentalized Sabbatarianism, Emerson was very much the Puritan. The Protestant ethic loomed high in his thought. In *Nature*, he asserted that "a man is fed, not that he may be fed, but that he may work." He admired the economic virtues—diligence, thrift, temperance, sobriety, and frugality—and tended to think that moral character and worldly achievement were closely related. He advised young people to "do their thing," but by it he meant "do their work," that is, find their calling and work hard at developing their native gifts. He came close at times to thinking that riches and godliness were allied, and he once upset Alcott by saying too many fine things about wealth in one of his lectures. But Emerson was no simple apologist for bourgeois wealth. He thought the pursuit of wealth for its own sake silly and degrading. (One of his ancestors, according to his aunt Mary Moody Emerson, "prayed every night that none of his descendants might ever be rich.") He also deplored the narrowness, meanness, bigotry, and ultraconservatism of wealthy men in his own day. "No land is bad," he once wrote, "but land is worse. If a man own land, the land owns him." There was law for man and law for thing, he said in his "Ode Inscribed to W. H. Channing," and the former, which expressed itself in love, friendship, truth, and virtue, was superior to the latter, which was embodied in material goods. Emerson also praised poverty, but for Puritan reasons: it excluded people from sensual enjoyment and directed their activities into safe and right channels (as it undoubtedly had in his own case when he was young and poor).

The Puritan influence on Emerson's aesthetic views was also powerful, though he strove hard to rise above it. It was difficult for him to think of art divorced from morality. Though he did at times voice the opinion that beauty was its own excuse for being, he usually placed the moral sentiment highest in his value system and thought of the poet as basically a moralist. "As soon as beauty is sought . . . for pleasure," he wrote, "it degrades the seeker." In his essay "Art," he insisted that "Art has not yet come to its maturity if it do not put itself abreast with the most potent influences of the world, if it is not practical and moral, if it do not stand in connection with conscience. . . ." As a young man, he was bothered by the impurities he found in Shakespeare, and as an adult he found it hard to accept Byron and Goethe because of their self-indulgent behavior. Goethe was his biggest problem, partly because his friends Thomas Carlyle and Margaret Fuller were fervent Goethe admirers and partly because he recognized Goethe's genius. In a letter to Carlyle in November, 1834, he expressed qualified admiration for Goethe, but criticized the "velvet life" he led and said that "the Puritan in me accepts no apology for bad morals in such as *he*. . . ." He came eventually, under Carlyle's tutelage, to acknowledge Goethe's greatness and devoted a chapter to him in *Representative Men*, but he was never completely reconciled (nor was Parker) to "our wise, but sensual" Goethe. (Ironically, Emerson himself offended Lane by serving wine to guests and shocked Alcott by using vivid language from everyday life in one of his lectures.)

Margaret Fuller probably freed herself from the Puritan imperatives she learned as a girl more than any other Transcendentalist. Though she, too, had reservations at first about Goethe's character, she stoutly defended his writings against charges of depravity and insisted that for all his moral peccadilloes the books he wrote represented "an unbroken series of efforts to develop the higher elements of being." It was wrong, she said, to "ignore or *annihilate*" the material side of man. "That is the real life which is subordinated to, not merged in, the ideal," she wrote; "*he is only wise who can bring the lowest act of his life into sympathy with its highest thought.*" Her main complaint about Goethe was not his mistresses; it was his fawning behavior in the presence of royalty, which, in an article for *The Dial*, she contrasted unfavorably with the proud and independent spirit of Beethoven, another hero of hers. She enjoyed quoting Beethoven's scornful description of how Goethe bowed and scraped before members of the imperial family while he stood proud, defiant, sturdy, and erect and was rewarded by their attention and respect.

Henry Thoreau was one with Margaret Fuller in resisting the moralizing tendencies of the day, though the two had little else in common. "The best thought," wrote Thoreau in January, 1841, "is not only without sombreness, but even without morality." Life itself transcended petty moral categories, Thoreau came to believe, and the preacher had to be silent about our deepest experiences and highest reaches of thought. "The conscience," he exclaimed, "really does not, and ought not to monopolize the whole of our lives, any more than the heart or the head. It is as liable to disease as any other part." Like any good Transcendentalist, he spiritualized the material world, but he was reluctant to identify natural and moral law the way Emerson did. He also had serious reservations about the Puritan work ethic, which he thought subordinated living to laboring and made man an alien in the universe. "The order of things should be somewhere reversed," he once exclaimed; "the seventh should be man's day of toil, wherein to earn his living by the sweat of his brow; and the other six his Sabbath of the affections and the soul, in which to range this widespread garden, and drink in the soft influences and sublime revelation of Nature." In his daily excursions into the great outdoors, Thoreau immersed himself in the welter of natural stimuli in a way that no other Transcendentalist did. His journal was a compendium of sights, sounds, odors, and tastes, and revealed a sensual awareness that few people ever achieve. In his writing, Thoreau struggled hard to subordinate the moralistic element. He had reached the conclusion that morality in art lay in the depth and intensity of life which the artist conveyed in his work and in his faithfulness to his materials.

Yet Thoreau, who never married, had his Puritanic side like all the Transcendentalists. He thought smoking was the habit of "vile men," shunned wine, tea, and coffee, and was enormously solemn about sex. He was deeply offended when Ellery Channing, the poetic nephew of the great preacher, told an off-color story and he wrote about it at length afterward. "The subject of sex," he said, "is one on which I do not wish to meet a man at all unless I *can* meet him on the most inspiring ground—if his view degrades and does not elevate. I would preserve purity in act and thought, as I would

cherish the memory of my mother." Though he praised
the Hindus for their frankness about sex, criticized false
modesty, and insisted that people recognize the animal
in their nature, he idealized sexual relations, thought
chastity conserved creative energy, and chided nature
for producing a fungus (*phallus impudicus*) that looked
like male genitals. ("What the essential difference between man and woman is," he once mused, "that they
should be thus attracted to one another, no one has
satisfactorily answered.")

But Puritan inhibition did not prevent Thoreau—or
Emerson or Alcott—from appreciating the poetic genius
of Walt Whitman, the earthy Brooklyn Transcendentalist who wrote freely about his sexual feelings. It was
Emerson who discovered Whitman. When Whitman
sent him a copy of *Leaves of Grass* (1855), Emerson read it
with mounting excitement: here, he decided, was the
kind of authentic American poetry for which he had
called in his Phi Beta Kappa address almost twenty years
before. In a letter acknowledging the "wonderful gift"
Whitman had sent him, Emerson called the book "the
most extraordinary piece of wit and wisdom that
America has yet contributed" and exclaimed: "I greet
you at the beginning of a great career. . . ." He was
somewhat disconcerted when Whitman quoted from his
letter on the cover of the second edition of *Leaves*, but not
enough to lose interest in him. He journeyed to Brooklyn
to meet Whitman, arranged for publication of some of
Whitman's verse in New England magazines, and kept in
touch with him for a number of years thereafter. Emerson had reservations about Whitman's frank sensuality.
(Respectable people were shocked by *Leaves*: Whittier
threw his copy into the fire and when Emerson wanted to
take Whitman to the Saturday Club, Longfellow, Lowell,
and Holmes said they had no desire to meet him.) "There
are parts of the book," he confessed, "where I hold my

nose as I read," but he had no fears that "any man who has eyes in his head will fail to see the genius in these poems." At one meeting between the two on Boston Common, Emerson urged Whitman to omit some passages from the next edition of *Leaves* because he thought the book would do better without "its sex handicap." But he accepted without further argument Whitman's insistence that he could not do so without violating his aesthetic conscience.

In November, 1856, Alcott, who had already met and liked Whitman for his brute power and audacity, took Thoreau to Brooklyn for a meeting. Thoreau and Whitman did not hit it off well; Thoreau's genteel reserve and Whitman's natural heartiness made them both feel uncomfortable. But Thoreau was impressed; he found Whitman "remarkably strong though coarse" and, despite his rough exterior, essentially a gentleman. After reading the copy of *Leaves* that Whitman gave him, Thoreau reported that "it has done me more good than any reading for a long time." Like Emerson, he was dismayed by some things in the book. "There are two or three pieces in the book," he told a friend, "which are disagreeable, to say the least; simply sensual. He does not celebrate love at all. It is as if the beasts spoke." Still, he went on to say, he found the poems exhilarating. "As for its sensuality,—I do not so much wish that those parts were not written, as that men and women were so pure that they could read them without harm, that is, without understanding them. One woman told me that no woman could read it,—as if a man could read what a woman could not. . . ." There would always be mutual reservations on the part of both Whitman and the Concord group. Whitman admired Emerson ("I was simmering, simmering, simmering; Emerson brought me to a boil") but was vexed by his "cold and bloodless intellectuality." And Emerson acknowledged Whitman's "real inspiration," but thought it was "choked by Titanic abdomen."

Moral and Scientific Absolutism

In their moral absolutism, as well as in their Puritan gentility, the Transcendentalists were very much the children of their age. Transcendentalism, announced Parker grandly, "appeals to a natural justice, natural right; absolute justice, absolute right." John Quincy Adams, who regarded Transcendentalism as ineffable nonsense, was a moral absolutist; so was that Transcendentalist-baiter Andrews Norton and that wild man from Tennessee Andrew Jackson. The Transcendentalists never doubted that the "higher law" to which they appealed far surpassed the principles guiding most Americans; yet their affirmation of eternal principles was as old as the Pilgrim settlement at Plymouth and older. The seventeenth-century Puritans, however, turned to the Scriptures for eternal verities while the Transcendentalists looked to the "moral sense." They did not realize how modern the concept of an intuitive moral sense was. The belief that human beings possess a special sense (or sentiment) which perceives distinctions between right and wrong was, in fact, largely the creation of English and Scottish moralists, beginning with the Earl of Shaftesbury (1671-1713) and Francis Hutcheson (1694-1746), who sought trustworthy moral guidelines within the human mind to replace waning ecclesiastical, theological, and Scriptural authority. Kant himself stressed reason as the ultimate moral authority and poured scorn on the belief that there was a special faculty of the mind called the moral sense. "As to moral faculty, this supposed special sense," he wrote, "the appeal to it is indeed superficial when those who cannot *think* believe that feeling will help them out, even in what concerns general laws." Yet Kant reasoned himself into moral principles as absolute as anything discerned by the moral sense or by the Transcendentalists' Puritan forebears. Every influence on the Transcendentalists—Kant, Scottish philosophy, Puritanism—predisposed them to think that their principles were absolute and unconditioned and not shaped by social and historical experience.

Like all moral absolutists, the Transcendentalists suffered from overconfidence in their ability to transcend circumstances and burst the bonds of class and region. The appeal to "spiritual laws" transcending time and place unquestionably sharpened their social criticism, and it surely accounted for their militant abolitionism in the 1850's. But the apostles of the Newness were never so universalistic in practice as they imagined they were (nor, of course, were their non-Transcendental contemporaries). Like most Americans, they tended to talk like Kantians and act like Lockeans. The Transcendentalists did not succeed in shucking off all the prejudices of their class—distrust of Catholics, disdain for Irish immigrants, impatience with the ordinary uneducated American, and reservations about the ability of blacks—though they did far better than most New Englanders. In principle, of course, they accepted the divinity of all men and women; in practice, they thought some people were diviner than others. (Whitman's faith in the "divine average" made him the most consistent Transcendentalist.) For all his genuine humaneness, Emerson sometimes displayed a remarkable callousness when discussing people about whom he had no direct knowledge. In "The Tragic" (1844), for example, he pointed out that a tender American girl was naturally shocked by the horrors of the "middle passage" and might be inclined to doubt the goodness of God. But she should never doubt, Emerson declared, for

* * *

to such as she these crucifixions do not come; they
come to the obtuse and barbarous, to whom they are
not horrid, but only a little worse than the old suffer-
ings. They exchange a cannibal war for the stench of
the hold. They have gratifications which would be
none to the civilized girl.

How Emerson could know this, he did not say; he was
defending a general point (the goodness of creation),
and his reasoning overwhelmed his humanity. Thoreau
did somewhat better. Though he had the New En-
glander's typical distrust of the Irish, he did come to
know and like some of them. His penchant for the concrete (though, like Emerson, he also liked facts to flower
into abstract truths) stood him in good stead in this
instance. But most of the Transcendentalists, when discussing grand principles, forgot that general principles
by themselves do not suffice in human relations and that
piecemeal knowledge gained by direct, immediate, sensitive, face-to-face contacts is also essential for developing
civilized behavior. They also seemed not to realize that
universal principles are inevitably narrowed down
whenever made use of and that something important is
always omitted when they are applied to concrete situations; and that, further, without the restraints learned
from existential encounter, the moral absolutist, blind or
indifferent to his exclusions, tends to turn hard and
cruel.

It would be unfair to press the point; the Transcendentalists were not normally heartless, and they were
probably better than most of their contemporaries in
their humane leanings and in their ability to rise above
the parochial prejudices of their time and place. Yet for
all their appeal to moral absolutes, they had some of the
same limitations in outlook that all educated New Englanders possessed during the Age of Jackson. Their

desire, moreover, to encourage self-transcendent rather than self-assertive behavior on the part of individuals, while noble in intent, showed a certain blindness to realities. It did not occur to them—it rarely does to absolutists—that self-transcendence can be as dangerous and destructive as self-aggrandizement. As Arthur Koestler has pointed out, the crimes resulting from selfish behavior by individuals are negligible compared to those committed by people acting out of self-sacrificing devotion on behalf of true religion, just policy, or correct ideology. It is only fair to add, however, that Emerson, who sooner or later saw every side of an issue, realized this, too. "I know very well," he once wrote, "that it is a bad sign in a man to be too conscientious and stick at gnats. The most desperate scoundrels have been the over-refiners. Without accommodation society is impracticable." Still, the Transcendentalists had a fondness for immutable morality and a distrust of the accommodative that stemmed from their Puritan background.

The Transcendentalists tended to be scientific absolutists as well as moral absolutists, and in this they were also very much of their times. Though they saw creation as pervaded with spiritual energy and in perpetual flux, they did not entirely free themselves from the Newtonian clockwork view of the universe with its static, invariant laws. Transcendentalists like Emerson looked upon scientific laws as eternal and immutable, not, as many scientists do today, as statistical generalizations about reality; they also thought of science itself as a body of fixed truths discovered by man rather than as an experimental method for establishing generalizations about empirical data with a high degree of probability, not absolute certainty. Their scientific outlook, in short, was pre-Darwinian; *Origin of Species* (1859) came too late to produce serious modifications in their Newtonianism, though some of them did begin to get a feel for Darwin-ian evolution later in life. The fact that Darwinism, when its implications became apparent, shattered the fixities and finalities of two thousand years of Western thought passed them entirely by, as it did most of their contem-poraries. It was not until most of the Transcendentalists had passed from the scene that philosophers, substitut-ing a Darwinian for a Newtonian universe, began to see change and growth, not immutability, as the chief characteristic of reality, to look on mind, not as a fixed entity, but as a dynamic instrument of comprehension, adjustment, and survival, and on ideas themselves, not as absolute transcripts of reality, but as provisional for-mulas for putting human beings into satisfactory relations with their environment.

From the post-Newtonian point of view, "cause" was not a transcendental form, intuited by the mind, as the Transcendentalists, following Kant, assumed, but rather a mental construct developed by human beings to ex-plain motion and change in the universe. But the concept of causality has lost a great deal of its usefulness since Emerson's day. The twentieth-century scientist saw little justification for breaking up happenings in the world into isolated events, grouping them in pairs, and then linking them together again in terms of cause and effect, for he had learned that changes in the world are too continuous in nature and too closely interwoven to be so treated. By the same token, he came to think of scientific law, not as sameness of causes and effects (as in the old days), but as sameness of relations, or, more precisely, as "sameness of differential equations" (as Bertrand Rus-sell put it) which were hard to express in non-mathematical language. The uniformity of nature, moreover, no longer meant "same cause, same effect," as it had to Newtonians, but rather the empirical (not *a priori*) principle of the probable permanence of scientific laws. "All philosophers, of every school," wrote Russell in 1917,

> imagine that causation is one of the fundamental axioms of science, yet, oddly enough, in advanced science, such as gravitational astronomy, the word "cause" never occurs. . . . The Law of Causality, I believe, like much that passes among philosophers, is a relic of a bygone age, surviving like the monarchy, only because it is erroneously supposed to do no harm.

As to time and space, they, too, lost their status in the twentieth century as intuitive Kantian forms with absolute validity; they were brought together into a four-dimensional space-time continuum in which events (not objects) were located. In the early twentieth century, Einstein showed that measurements of time and space were "relative" to some arbitrarily chosen frame of reference and that a clock in motion keeps time more slowly than a stationary one. It would be silly of course to condemn the Transcendentalists (and their contemporaries) for possessing naive notions about time, space, causality, and scientific law (though the case is far otherwise with the present generation of Americans), for these were part of the established wisdom of their day. What needs to be noted is that despite the Newtonian absolutes shaping his thought, Emerson was able on occasion to burst their bounds. He had a marvelous feeling for the endless flux of things and he realized that there was no truth "so sublime but it may be trivial tomorrow in the light of new thoughts" and that "not a piece of science but its flank may be turned tomorrow." He would have welcomed, one cannot doubt, the broader, richer, and more sophisticated view that twentieth-century physics has taken of the universe, for he was always open to new

ideas and a fresh look at reality. (He would have been
charmed, too, to know that some twentieth-century
physicists thought there was a subjective tinge to our
knowledge of the universe and that reality was ultimately
mental in nature.) On the other hand, his persistent
monistic bent impelled him to seek certainty rather than
probability in an ever-changing world and his angle of
vision remained to the end more Newtonian than Darwinian.

Absolutism in science inevitably produced universal
determinism in thinkers like Emerson. Emerson was an
astonishingly rigid determinist considering his repeated
calls for individual self-reliance and creativity. He absolutely barred all chance from his universe. The possibility that chance—a "blank and shapeless agency" and a
"blind lord of the changes that take place"—might in-
trude itself into the Transcendental world was simply
intolerable to him. As a young man he expressed what
was to be a lifelong view:

He who believes that Chance created the Universe,
and may shortly demolish it, that he is himself here
only by a lucky accident, and that no unseen Mind
has measured his progress or appointed his end,
must often, in his dark hours of weariness or distress
feel that he is alone and sink under the disgust of his
uncomfortable solitude. It is a desolate belief which
converts into a wilderness the great and blooming
garden of nature; which, by depriving things and
beings of object and utility, deprives them of the
very principle of beauty. . . . But add to this Universe
an Omniscient Governor and you have infused a
soul into the mighty mass. . . . You feel at once *secure*
. . . . The march of events which was loose and fortuitous becomes dignified and divine.

For Emerson it was an either/or choice: universal determinism or absolute tychism. He did not entertain the possibility that regularity and chance might coexist. He could feel at home in the universe only if he was sure that all events were bound together by an adamantine chain and that nothing capricious, fortuitous, whimsical, and accidental ever took place in it. He carried his determinism to extraordinary lengths. Everything happened, he insisted, at precisely its appointed time and place; there was a reason for all the contingencies of experience. Columbus appeared on the scene when it was time to discover America. "When Nature has work to be done, she creates a genius to do it." Newton was born when it was time for physics to take a big step forward; not only that, Newton's life style was fitted to his profession. "Nature protects her own work. To the culture of the world an Archimedes, a Newton is indispensable; so she guards them by a certain aridity. If these had been good fellows, fond of dancing, port and clubs, we should have had no Theory of the Sphere and no Principia." Each individual has a vocation and a position in the grand scheme of things and his character and fortunes are indissolubly linked. There is no rent in the seamless fabric of things.

No sooner is the electric telegraph devised than the gutta-percha, the very material it requires, is found. The aeronaut is provided with gun-cotton, the very fuel he wants for his balloon. When commerce is vastly enlarged, California and Australia expose the gold it needs. When Europe is over-populated, America and Australia crave to be peopled; and so throughout, every chance is time, as if Nature, who made the lock, knew where to find the key.

By seeing it all as the working of a beneficent necessity,

Emerson escaped an enervating fatalism. Yet his determinism was as complete as that of any Calvinist, and it was also inconsistent with his very real belief that freedom (as intellectual and moral insight producing transcendence) was an important human possibility. An insight that is fated to happen is hardly free. Nor is it especially true, valuable, or beautiful; it simply is. It pops up when its time has come. There was something tautological in all of Emerson's deterministic pronouncements.

But Emerson, fortunately, was not very consistent in any of this. When he wanted to emphasize fate, he did so forcefully; when he wanted to assert freedom, he also did so with assurance. He rarely bothered to confront the logical difficulties into which his reasoning led him. In Emersonian Transcendentalism, the tension between fate and freedom remained unresolved to the end, as, perhaps, in some respects, it always must. Because Transcendentalism accepted Newtonian physics as final, it was never able to bridge the gap between its faith in free human possibilities and its belief that everything in the world was causally related and interconnected down to the last grain of sand. With Darwinism, however, it became clear that chance, as well as uniform behavior, played a major role in the development of life. Darwinism's basic law, natural selection (which Emerson never thoroughly understood), was a generalization about myriads of fortuitous encounters between individual organisms and their environing conditions, which, after Darwin, was refined into a statement of statistical probabilities. After the Civil War, Charles S. Peirce, a physicist who was also to some extent a Transcendentalist, took a statistical view of all scientific law, which became authoritative for many in the twentieth century. The laws of nature, he pointed out, were approximate, not absolute, regularities, and they operated with a high degree of probability rather than invariantly. This meant that individual facts always departed to some extent from the laws governing their behavior and that chance and novelty played a real part in the universe. As a limited indeterminist, Peirce argued that mechanical determinism accounted neither for evolutionary development and increasing diversity in the world nor for the spontaneity involved in mental action. He was almost alone in his day in recognizing the statistical character of Darwin's law of natural selection, and he also anticipated the twentieth-century physicist Werner Heisenberg's principle of indeterminacy, according to which it is possible to generalize about the average behavior of multitudes of subatomic particles, but impossible to measure the precise behavior of single particles.

Today, the situation in physics is even more complicated than it was in Peirce's day (he died in 1914). Since the 1930's, physicists have isolated almost one hundred elementary particles as ultimate constituents of matter, including the positron, an electron that for a while moves backward in time. Moreover, in quantum physics, the principle of complementarity ascribes to subatomic particles a dualism—the capacity to behave both as particles and as waves—which Emerson and his contemporaries would have found mystifying. And in the supergalactic as well as in the subatomic realm, contemporary science continues to undergo a radical transformation in its understanding of the physical world that would have bewildered scientists in Emerson's day. There is no question that the kind of scientific outlook that the Transcendentalists accepted as authoritative and made part of their own thinking has been superseded by a far more complex and sophisticated world view.

* * *

Individuality, Creativity, and Sociality

The Transcendentalists, happily, were not systematizers; they did not weld their ideas into such a rigid mold that the collapse of one of them invalidated all the others. If in their Puritanism and in their moral and scientific absolutism they seem dated, in other respects they speak very much to the present. In their view of the individual and his relations to the natural and social environment, as well as in their aspirations for high culture and authentic living, they speak to thoughtful and sensitive people in every time and place. A society lacking the leaven of Transcendentalism is dreary indeed.

The Transcendentalists' emphasis on individuality probably has the support of modern science, if that is needed. "Nature," said Emerson, "never rhymes her children, nor makes two men alike." Variation seems to be a fundamental characteristic of creation. In the *Origin of Species*, Darwin devoted considerable space to describing the immense variety cropping up among living organisms. The chromosomes never reproduce themselves exactly; no two blades of grass are ever precisely alike (as Whitman recognized in his own poetic fashion in *Leaves of Grass*). "One leaf, one blade of grass, one meridian does not resemble another," said Emerson. "Every mind is different; and the more it is unfolded, the more pronounced is that difference." There seems, too, to be an irreducible individuality in the behavior of subatomic particles if we take Heisenberg seriously; and even the rotation of the earth is somewhat erratic. It is not necessary to put it this way, of course; the Transcendental insistence on the uniqueness of each human being might be compelling without the support of modern biology and physics. Still, the Transcendentalists placed great emphasis on the individual's relation to nature, and they always sought support for their views in the natural sciences. The Transcendental way of putting it was this: each man and woman is a special individuation of the basic divine energy at a given time and place in this universe and each has therefore a unique part to play in the grand theater of life. The individual should be independent and self-reliant; he should come to understand wherein his own individuality lies and to develop his own particular gifts in a fruitful fashion. He should also learn to be true to himself; self-knowledge, candor, courage, and integrity are all essential to realizing one's true individuality. In saying these things, the Transcendentalists may have overestimated the possibilities of individual autonomy. Yet the hope and promise they offered for individual growth add to the zest of life and are indispensable in any viable and creative community.

The Transcendentalists quite properly linked individuality with creativity. The power of social habit in shaping individuals is, to be sure, enormous, and perhaps they underestimated it when it came to artistic inspiration. Yet the individual, as they recognized, remains the source of variation, novelty, and originality, and the creative act is indisputably an individual act. Society may stimulate, shape, modify, ignore, and repress the creative act, but it can never originate one. The Transcendentalists realized this, and they gave every encouragement they could to individual creativity. They were exhilarated by the productions of genius (Plato, Shakespeare, Goethe, Beethoven), but they were also grateful for the accomplishments of talent (Wordsworth, Coleridge, Carlyle). They thought that the United States of their day discouraged creative expression, especially in the arts, and they wanted to liven up the cultural scene. (Emerson said that between 1790 and 1820 "there was not a book, a speech, a conversation, or a thought" in Massachusetts.) They also thought that promising young people probably suppressed their creative urges from fear of ridicule, disdain, even ostracism, on the part of their elders, and they wanted to assure these talented young of their moral support. In their appeals for creative independence, the Transcendentalists were also undoubtedly anxious to justify the dissatisfactions they themselves felt with American culture and to develop self-confidence in the expression of their own heresies.

The Transcendentalists surely did better with the act of creation than their Lockean contemporaries. In the twentieth century it came to be generally recognized (except among behaviorists) that intuition was a major source of creativity. In *Mysticism and Logic* (1917), Bertrand Russell acknowledged the intuitive source of scientific ideas as well as of artistic inspiration and religious mysticism. "Instinct, intuition, or insight is what first leads to the beliefs which subsequent reason confirms or confutes. . . ," he declared. "Reason is a harmonising, controlling force rather than a creative one." Unlike the Lockeans, the Transcendentalists were aware of unconscious mental processes long before Freud; Emerson thought that the "Unconscious," as he called it, was the source of "genius and virtue." The concept of an Unconscious was not original with Emerson (nor with Freud). As Lancelot Whyte has shown in *The Unconscious before Freud* (1960), it developed slowly in Western thought after Descartes (1596-1650) chose awareness as the defining characteristic of the human mind, thus ignoring factors (long taken for granted) lying outside of but influencing immediate awareness. By Emerson's time the insistence on unconscious mentation, especially among the Romantics, was becoming commonplace and Emerson found much confirmation in writers like Coleridge and Schelling for his own belief in preconscious cerebration. Unlike Russell and Freud, Transcendentalists like Emerson gave the unconscious or intuitive source of individual creativity the highest authority they could by presenting it as essentially a divine act. Its ultimate source, they said, was Universal Mind, which tried to get through to the individual by means of his intuitive Reason. By giving creative insight a divine foundation, the Transcendentalists hoped to persuade young people to take their creative stirrings seriously, to look forward with expectancy to the flashes of insight that may come sooner or later to everyone, and to nourish, rather than dismiss as mere vagaries, the wayward ideas that welled up in their consciousness. (Darwin once said that he had learned to stop brushing aside as preposterous the unconventional ideas that crossed his mind, for he had discovered that it was precisely these ideas which turned out, upon analysis, to have the greatest value in his inquiries.)

Many, perhaps most, people will find the Transcendental explanation for creativity unacceptable, but modern psychology has not really done much better with it. Consider, for example, the description of the creative process given by contemporary behaviorist psychology, which is based on stimulus-response theory and regards the terms "mind," "imagination," "consciousness," and "purpose," as unscientific. To the question of how we may account for the production of great works of literature, J. B. Watson, father of American behaviorism, declared in *Behaviorism* (1924) that *"we get them by manipulating words, shifting them about until a new pattern is hit upon,"* in the same way that a dress designer builds a new gown:

He calls his model in, picks up a new piece of silk, throws it around her; he pulls it in here, he pulls it out there, makes it tight or loose at the waist, high or low, he makes the skirt long or short. He manipulates the material until it takes on the semblance of a

dress. . . . Not until the new creation aroused admiration and condemnation, both his own . . . and
others', would manipulation be complete. . . .

Watson concluded his account of dress-designing by saying that it was "the equivalent of a rat's finding food" and
by adding: "The painter plies his trade in the same way,
nor can the poet boast of any other method." Reading
Watson, it is difficult not to feel that the Transcendentalists, with their recognition of the crucial part that
subconscious mentation plays in the creative act, were
closer to the truth than the behaviorists with their "rat-
omorphic" explanations. And surely Parker's effort to
describe the process, previously cited, is closer to empirical reality than Watson's: "We labour upon a thought,
trying to grasp the truth. We almost have the butterfly in
our hands, but cannot get it. Again we try; it will not
come; we walk, sit, pray, it will not come. At last in some
moment it flashes on us, the crystal forms, the work is all
done."

If the Transcendentalists were particularly concerned
with individual creativity, they never thought of the individual as acting in isolation from his natural and social
environments. "Do you not see," Emerson exclaimed,
"that a man is a bundle of relations, that his entire
strength consists not in his properties but in his innumerable relations?" In their emphasis on the individual's
organic relation to nature (a major theme in Transcendentalism), proponents of the New Views penetrated to
another permanent truth about human existence. The
individual, they recognized, is continuous with his environment; he is perpetually interacting with the physical
world. He continually absorbs oxygen, food, and sunshine from the natural world and at the same time endlessly transforms the natural vitalities encompassing him
as he does so. Nature, as Emerson put it, is flesh of our

flesh and bone of our bone; it is the circumstance that dwarfs all other circumstances. "We nestle in nature," he said, "and draw our living as parasites from her roots and grains"; our lives are "intertwined with the whole chain of organic and inorganic being." In its ministry to man, he added, nature "is not only the material but also the process and the result." Thoreau put it more rhapsodically. "Of thee, O earth," he cried, "are my bone and sinew made; to thee, O sun, am I brother.... To this dust my body will gladly return as to its origin. Here have I my habitat. I am of thee." The Transcendentalists celebrated man's capacity for transmuting natural energies into practical instruments for his own benefit; but they also celebrated the beauty, majesty, and awesome power of the natural world. Indeed, Thoreau's reverence for nature became at times sacramental. "Nature does her best to feed man. . . ," he once wrote.

> We pluck and eat in remembrance of Her. It is a sacrament, a communion. Our bread need not ever be sour or hard to digest. What Nature is to the mind she is also to the body. As she feeds my imagination, she will feed my body; for what she says she means, and is ready to do. She is not simply beautiful to the poet's eye. Not only the rainbow and sunset are beautiful, but to be fed and clothed, sheltered and warmed aright, are equally beautiful and inspiring.

Thoreau's feeling of kinship with nature was so profound that on occasion he achieved a state of consciousness in which he felt totally absorbed into the natural processes environing him. He was shocked by the reckless depredations of man into the natural world, and toward the end of his life he became seriously interested in the conservation of natural resources.

The Transcendentalists placed man squarely in the

midst of nature, and though they unquestionably over-
rated its beneficence, they did not make the mistake of
seeing the two in perpetual conflict. They never denied
the importance of science and technology in harnessing
natural forces for human uses. They did insist, however,
that the aesthetic side of nature was of equal importance
to man; wonder, not just plunder, should characterize
the human view of the natural world. The Transcendental respect for the natural universe (which may possibly
be renewed as urban man extends his excursions farther
and farther into outer space) shone forth brightly in a
passage Thoreau wrote in his journal on Christmas Day,
1852:

> I, standing twenty miles off, see a crimson cloud in
> the horizon. You tell me it is a mass of vapor which
> absorbs all other rays and reflects the red, but that is
> nothing to the purpose, for this red vision excites
> me, stirs my blood, makes my thoughts flow, and I
> have new and indescribable fancies, and you have
> not touched the secret of that influence. If there is
> not something mystical in your explanation, some-
> thing unexplainable to the understanding, some
> elements of mystery, it is quite insufficient. If there
> is nothing in it which speaks to my imagination, what
> boots it? What sort of science is that which enriches
> the understanding, but robs the imagination? . . . If
> we knew all things thus mechanically merely, should
> we know anything really?

The Transcendentalists realized that the qualitative
world of the poet was just as real as the quantitative world
of the scientist. They knew something, too, of what
Freud called the "oceanic feeling," that is, the expansion
of awareness, sense of awe and wonder, and feeling of
oneness with the universe which is the source of religious

mysticism, pure science, and high art. (Einstein believed that a person who had no capacity for wonder "might just as well be dead for he has already closed his eyes upon life.") Parker's view was typical:

> To me, human life in all its forms, individual and aggregate, is a perpetual wonder; the flora of the earth and sea is full of beauty and of mystery which science seeks to understand; the fauna of land and ocean is not less wonderful; the world which holds them both, and the great universe that folds it on every side, are still more wonderful, complex, and attractive, to the contemplative mind. But the universe of human life, with its peculiar worlds of outer sense and inner soul, . . . are still more complex, wonderful, and attractive; and the laws which control it seem to me more amazing than the mathematical principles that explain the celestial mechanics of the outer world.

The Transcendentalists were insistent on the social as well as the natural side of the individual. Though they placed a high valuation on self-reliant and creative individualism, they never glorified the selfish impulses of the individual acting for himself alone. "The individual alone is a wild man," said Parker; "it is only in society that noble individualism is . . . possible." John S. Dwight put it this way: "No man is himself, *alone*. Part of me is in you, in every fellow being. We 'live and move and have our being' in one another, as well as in God. An individual is nothing in himself. . . . We are real *persons* only entering into true relations with all other beings; we enter into our own lives and find ourselves just in proportion as we realize and make good those relations." The Transcendentalists were not "rugged" individualists. They thought of the individual as continuous with his social as

well as with his natural environment, and they warned
that if people behaved willfully and with disregard for
others, they lost their organic relation to the environment and thus their moral and spiritual health. Emerson
thought that excessive egotism was a disease something
like chorea, in which a person "runs round a ring formed
by his own talent, falls into an admiration of it, and loses
relation to the world." His remedy for the "goitre of
egotism" was broadening one's interests through art,
philosophy, religion, travel, and social contacts. "In the
procession of the soul from within outward," he wrote in
his essay "Love" (1841), "it enlarges its circles ever, like
the pebble thrown into the pond, or the light proceeding
from an orb." His essays, from the outset, were filled with
exhortations to the individual to free himself from ser-
vitude to particulars, to resist the "maxims of low prudence," and to seek public and universal ends. "That is
the best part of each writer," he said, "which has nothing
private in it. . . ." He sometimes spoke of the "general
mind" or "common mind" of humanity to which each
individual mind was related. Increasingly, as he grew
older and his religious affirmations became attenuated,
the mind which he thought of as common to all human
beings assumed an importance in his thinking rivaling
that of the Universal Mind pervading the cosmos.

Thoreau was, of course, more defiantly individualistic
than Emerson or any of the other Transcendentalists.
But his ethical norms were no more narrowly self-
interested than theirs. He had more scorn for rugged
economic individualism than Emerson (who could not
help admiring entrepreneurial as well as artistic
achievement), and he was utterly disdainful of the
utilitarian and materialistic standards which he thought
made Jacksonian America vulgar and mediocre. It was
precisely the low standards which he thought governed
American institutions that made him such a militant

social nonconformist and led him, on occasion, to express a preference for solitude over society and for nature over humanity. But when his high principles were directly challenged, as he thought they were by the Fugitive Slave Act, he could become as fervently active in the social arena as the next Transcendentalist. He believed, moreover, in collective action on the local level, particularly in the realm of education, and in *Walden* proposed that villages provide facilities for liberal studies:

> As the nobleman of cultivated taste surrounds himself with whatever conduces to his culture—genius—learning—wit—books—paintings—statuary—music—philosophical instruments and the like; so let the village do. . . . To act collectively is according to the spirit of our institutions. . . . Instead of noblemen, let us have noble villages of men.

He also wanted each town to set aside a park or forest for instruction and recreation.

None of the Transcendentalists was a socialist in any serious sense, not even Ripley, though many of them, including Emerson, had considerable sympathy for socialist idealism. Nor were any of them consistent social activists. But none of them was a reckless individualist. They possessed too much civility to be socially irresponsible, and they all possessed a strong sense of community. And they tried hard (though not always successfully) to include people outside the range of their normal associations within the orbit of their sympathies: blacks, Indians, Irish immigrants, idiosyncratic young people, Midwesterners, working people. "See this wide society of laboring men and women," exclaimed Emerson in the lecture "Man the Reformer" (1841).

We allow ourselves to be served by them, we live

apart from them, and meet them without a salute in the streets. We do not greet their talents, nor rejoice in their good fortune, nor foster their hopes, nor in the assembly of people vote for what is dear to them. Thus we enact the part of the selfish noble and king from the foundation of the world.

His solution may have been anticlimactic: "Let our affection flow out to our fellows; it would operate in a day the greatest of all revolutions." Still, he recognized the limitations that personal experience places on all people, and he was trying to break through them as best he could. The Transcendentalists were ever striving to broaden their horizons. They recognized that an individualism which lacked social content was futile and self-defeating. They also realized that no society is viable for long which does not manage a considerable degree of transcendence over rugged individualism. Civilization, they thought, required highly socialized as well as boldly self-reliant individuals.

High Culture and Creative Living

Civilization also required high culture. The measure of civilization, the Transcendentalists thought, lay not in a nation's size, strength, and economic well-being, but in the quality of its culture: its art, music, literature, philosophy, science, and religion. Emerson thought that culture was the "chief end of man" and that the problem of civilization was to make the "masterpieces of art and nature" available to everyone. The Transcendentalists labored hard, in their translations, anthologies, journals, lectures, books, and "Conversations," to make world masterpieces accessible to the American people. They tried, as Emerson put it, to be "collectors of the heavenly spark, with power to convey the electricity to others."

They thought social reform was important, but they denied its primacy in the scheme of civilized values; it was never an end in itself, but only a means for achieving a better society in which the arts and sciences could flourish freely. The vocation of the artist, they thought, was never to be subordinated to that of the reformer, and art itself was never to become mere propaganda. In his own way, they insisted, the creative artist contributed as much as, if not more than, the reformer to the advance of society, for without art there was no real civilization. When he helped found *The Dial* in 1840, Emerson was anxious to keep it out of the hands of both social reformers and scholarly pedants; its concern was with serious culture. *The Dial* did not entirely neglect reform; but it spent far fewer pages on Fourierism than it did on Shakespeare, Dante, Goethe, Michelangelo, Homer, Chaucer, Shelley, Kant, and Milton. Margaret Fuller, the first editor of *The Dial*, once said that the principal object of her life was "to introduce here the works of these great geniuses (of Europe), the flower and fruit of a higher state of development, which might give the young who are soon to constitute the state, a higher standard in thought and action than would be demanded of them by their own time."

The Transcendentalists thought that high culture nourished creativity. An individual's intuitive processes did not operate in a vacuum any more than the individual himself did; they needed something to work on. Fruitful insights in art, science, and religion came only to people who felt thoroughly at home in these fields and pondered them deeply on the conscious level. Knowledge, in other words, was as important to the Transcendentalists as intuition was. They did not believe that blissful ignorance or contented superficiality produced imaginative insight and they had no use for the ignorant man's opinion. America's hope, Margaret Fuller cried, lay "not in ignorance, but in knowledge." Emerson placed a high valuation on creative inspiration, but he did not think that untutored intuition would produce anything interesting, significant, or enlightening. Until people knew something worth knowing, their intuitions were not likely to be worth attending to. In America, Emerson feared, people tended to confuse uninformed opinion with creative insight, thus evading the hard work of mastering the knowledge and skills that were indispensable to all genuinely creative endeavor. "Because our education is defective," he lamented in 1857,

> because we are superficial and ill-read, we are forced to make the most of that position, of ignorance. Hence America is a vast know-nothing party, and we disparage books, and cry up intuition. With a few clever men we have made a reputable thing of that, and denouncing libraries and severe culture, and magnifying the mother-wit swagger of bright boys from the country colleges, we have even come so far as to deceive everybody, except ourselves, into an admiration of un-learning and inspiration, forsooth.

Knowledge without creative insight was deadening, but intuition without informed intelligence was fatuous. The Transcendentalists stressed intuition in order to unstiffen the arteriosclerotic thinking of the educated classes of their day; but they had not meant to replace learned men like Andrews Norton and Francis Bowen with a bunch of garrulous ignoramuses. "I am always happy," Emerson confessed, "to meet persons who perceive the transcendent superiority of Shakespeare over all other writers. I like people who like Plato." He added that if he were traveling "in the dreary wilderness of Arkansas or Texas" and discovered a man on the next seat reading

Horace, or Martial, or Calderón, "we would wish to hug him." The Transcendentalists did what they could to bring foreign masterpieces to the attention of the American people. Margaret Fuller, anxious to familiarize young Americans with European genius, wrote extensively about Goethe in *The Dial*, Frederic Hedge published an anthology of German prose writers, Christopher Cranch translated the *Aeneid*, John Dwight pushed the cause of Beethoven and other German composers in *Dwight's Journal of Music* (founded in 1852), George Ripley published translations of German and French writers in his *Specimens of Foreign Standard Literature*, Thoreau (an immensely learned man who thought the Greek classics should be read in the original) presented selections from the Oriental Scriptures in *The Dial*, and James Clarke did an influential study of the great world religions. The Transcendentalists broadened the outlook of educated Americans; they encouraged them to look beyond the horizon of English and classical art and literature.

The Transcendentalists were anxious to encourage artistic endeavor in the United States as well as develop a taste for the best in foreign art and literature. Properly understood, great foreign art did not, in their opinion, evoke imitation; it stimulated original expression on the part of native artists. The Transcendentalists did not disdain popular culture; insofar as it was fresh and vital and grew naturally out of folk experience, it met their criterion for authentic creation. They also realized that it was a major source for high art. What they objected to in art was the spurious, the derivative, the imitative; they thought American culture was stale and dull, and they wanted Americans to elevate their sights by coming to know the great works of other lands. They emphasized foreign genius partly as a means of stimulating genuine creative expression on the part of Americans themselves.

The Dial published young new writers, and Emerson was generous in his encouragement of youthful poets whom he found promising. But the Transcendentalists had their blind spots. Partly because of their Puritanism, most of them never took fiction seriously, and the achievements of Hawthorne and Melville (as well as Poe) passed them by. Whitman was their only important discovery. Furthermore, with the exception of Emerson and Thoreau, it cannot be said that the Transcendentalists themselves contributed anything of permanent value to world literature or even to American literature. Most of their writings have little intrinsic appeal; they are interesting chiefly as documents illustrating another stage in the emancipation of the American mind from its Puritan past, and their significance is historical, not aesthetic.

Emerson and Thoreau, however, made permanent contributions to American and to world literature, and their influence here and abroad has been persistent. John Dewey said that Emerson was "the one citizen of the New World fit to have his name uttered in the same breath with Plato." He may have exaggerated Emerson's standing as a philosopher, but surely not his standing as a poet, who in his verse and prose handled large ideas with verve and imagination and almost infinite suggestiveness and clothed them in language that is exalted in diction and breathtaking at times in imagery. Some of his essays ("Self-Reliance," "The American Scholar," "Fate") are among the best ever composed by an American writer. Friedrich Nietzsche, who liked Emerson's health, serenity, intellectual independence, and aristocratic grace, ranked him with the four best prose writers of the nineteenth century and, though he regretted his lack of discipline as a thinker, called him the "author as yet the richest in ideas of this century." Regarding Emerson as a "brother soul," Nietzsche carried a volume of Emerson essays with him when he traveled, filled his German editions of the essays with marginal notes and underlinings, and once exclaimed that Emerson had "absolutely no idea of how old he is already, and how young he will yet be. . . ." Thoreau, too, with *Walden* and the essay on civil disobedience, has added significantly to American and to world literature. Thoreau's case is in some ways more interesting than Emerson's. Emerson's work was recognized during his own lifetime, in England, France, and Germany, as well as in the United States, and after the Civil War he became a kind of American poet laureate. Thoreau was almost totally neglected by the public until his death in 1862. His first book, *A Week on the Concord and Merrimack Rivers*, was a worst-seller; it did so poorly that the publisher returned most of the copies to him. "I now have a library of nearly nine hundred volumes, over seven hundred of which I wrote myself," Thoreau reflected wryly. "Is it not well that the author should behold the fruits of his labor?" His second book, *Walden*, did somewhat better (2,000 copies sold in five years), and after Thoreau's death its reputation grew steadily. In the late nineteenth century the newly organized British Labour party used it as a kind of textbook, and in the twentieth century esteem for Thoreau came, to some extent, to exceed that for Emerson. Today countless editions of both *Walden* and the essay on civil disobedience are available in many languages.

The perennial appeal of the Transcendentalists has rested largely on their impassioned quest for noble ways of using the great gifts of life. The Transcendental revolt began in religion, and though it soon moved into other realms of life it remained essentially religious in its quest for meaning and purpose. It was at heart an effort to eliminate the false, artificial, meretricious, and stylized and to clear the way for an honest, direct, natural, and deeply felt response to the miracle of creation. Men and women have always sought to understand the universe so that they might harness its forces for practical purposes; but some of them, like the Transcendentalists, have wanted to do more than this: they have acknowledged their kinship with the great nonhuman world and sought to live as an intimate part of its marvelous throbbing energies. Transcendentalists like Emerson and Thoreau thought most people misused the gift of life. They lived, Thoreau said, lives of quiet desperation. They had no sense of oceanic wonder. They did not really feel at home in the universe, despite lip service to conventional ways of conceiving it, and they moved about frantically in an effort to disguise their bewilderment from themselves and from others. They sacrificed living (which puzzled them) to getting a living (which seemed safe and sure). On the farm they became serfs of the soil; in the factory they became machines and tools of tools; in the classroom they became pompous pedants. They thought of their work as a chore, not a sport. They cluttered their lives with needless luxuries and trivial details and took a thousand stitches today in order to save nine tomorrow. They seemed everywhere to be "doing penance in a thousand remarkable ways" and looked on their brief span of existence as a hardship rather than as a pastime. Worst of all, they never dreamed. "If you have built castles in the air, your work need not be lost," Thoreau insisted; "that is where they should be. Now put the foundations under them."

Thoreau went to Walden Pond in March, 1845, in order to discover whether, by stripping life down to its basic essentials, he could achieve a fruitful union of work and play, labor and leisure, getting a living and living. (Ripley sought the same objective at Brook Farm, Alcott at Fruitlands, and Emerson in Concord.) He enjoyed building his cabin, making furniture, raising beans, preparing food, and gathering fuel. He also proceeded

merrily with his real vocation: writing. He wrote most of
A Week and a large part of *Walden* while living at Walden
Pond. He took frequent trips to Concord (where, he said,
he was widely traveled) to see friends and even fre-
quenter trips into the countryside around the pond in
order to drench himself in the sounds, sights, tastes, and
scents of the hills, fields, woods, and waters around him.
He left Walden in September, 1847, because he had
other lives to live and could spare no more time for that
particular life. "We should come home from afar," he
said, "from adventures, and perils, and discoveries every
day, with new experience and character." Thoreau's disdain for the compulsive work ethic aroused suspicion,
indignation, and hostility in respectable people, but he
refused to be intimidated. He was a competent surveyor,
and he could have been a successful businessman in his
father's pencil-making business (he developed a flotation
process for graphite that proved profitable), but he preferred to be an "inspector of snow-storms and rain-
storms" and a chronicler of his experiences in the natural
world. Even Emerson did not fully understand him. But
then none of the Transcendentalists fully understood
each other; nor was there any need for them to do so. "If
a man does not keep pace with his companion," wrote
Thoreau in *Walden*, "perhaps it is because he hears a
different drummer. Let him step to the music which he
hears, however measured or far away."

Other temperaments, other lives. Emerson differed
considerably in character and personality from
Thoreau, and his life was quite otherwise than that of his
Walden friend. He enjoyed trips into fields and forests
the way Thoreau did, but he decided early that he was no
handyman and that it was not intended that "the writer
should dig." He enjoyed a bit of wine at the dinner table,
belonged to Boston's prestigious Saturday Club, and
after the Civil War, when his countrymen began trans-

forming him from iconoclast into icon, he was elected to the Harvard Board of Overseers. (Thoreau had many lives to live but none of them in a clubhouse or college board room.) Emerson was surely closer to respectability than Thoreau, and he did not inspect snowstorms or lead huckleberry parties the way his young friend did. Nevertheless, he was unquestionably one with Thoreau on essentials. Both regarded the choice of vocation as momentous; both looked upon life as a precious boon; and both thought of the present (which Emerson called the Everlasting Now) as sacred ground. In 1858, Emerson noted delightedly in his journal that Thoreau "thought nothing to be hoped from you, if this bit of mould under your feet was not sweeter for you to eat than any other in this world, or in any world."

From the beginning of his Transcendental career, Emerson, like Thoreau, had wanted men and women to make Waldens of their lives. "The sun shines today also," he reminded them in *Nature*. "There is more wool and flax in the fields. There are new lands, new men, new thoughts. Let us demand our own works and laws and worship." We impoverish our lives, Emerson thought, if we see and hear only with our memories, never with our eyes and ears, or if we focus exclusively on intentions and prospects and ignore the "enveloping Now." We must "live for ourselves. . . ," he declared, "and not as the pall-bearers of a funeral, but as upholders and creators of our age. . . ." We must learn to appreciate the piquancy of the present. We must come to know that today is a king in disguise and that we may unmask him as he passes. The perpetual admonition of nature to us, Emerson said, is this: "The world is new, untried. Do not believe the past. I give you the universe a virgin today." We must husband our moments, fill the hours, become lord of the day. "He only is rich who owns the day," exclaimed Emerson. The days "come and go like muffled and veiled figures, sent from a distant and friendly party; but they say nothing and if we do not use the gifts they bring, they carry them as silently away." We delude ourselves if we do not think that the present hour is the critical and decisive one. No yesterday and no tomorrow can be so crucial for us as today is; we must stop our perpetual remembering and postponing. "Write it on your heart," said Emerson, "that every day is the best day of the year. No man has learned anything rightly until he knows that every day is Doomsday."

No one, as George Santayana remarked, can be a Transcendentalist all of the time. Human beings are necessarily both retrospective and prospective in outlook, and they have plans, purposes, commitments, and opportunities to take account of as well as Waldens to explore. But no one can be said to feel truly at home in the universe who is not a Transcendentalist at least some of the time. Life becomes exhilarating, Emerson wrote in "Works and Days," when we suspend our relentless anatomizing of it, rise above our linguistic categorizations, and, for the moment, try to experience its music and magic directly and spontaneously. "You must treat the days respectfully," he advised, "you must be a day yourself. . . . You must hear the bird's song without attempting to render it into nouns and verbs." Beyond the implacable customs, imposing bureaucracies, and prestigious ideologies that hem us in, according to the Transcendentalists, lie the essential miracle, majesty, and mystery of creation. They were convinced that a fresh sense of wonder at it all from time to time would renew us, give us health and youth and joy, and enable us to move on in the toilsome journey of life as freer and wiser men and women.

In 1859, when he was fifty-five, Emerson noted with satisfaction that after twenty-five years of writing and speaking he had not a single disciple because he had wished to bring people to themselves, not to him. John Tyndall, a British physicist who adored Emerson, once remarked that Emerson put so much emphasis on independence in his essays that his most devoted readers felt almost honor-bound to pick quarrels with him. "The best part of Emersonianism," said Whitman, "is, it breeds the giant that destroys itself. Who wants to be any man's mere followers? lurked behind every page. No teacher ever taught, that has so provided for his pupil's setting up independently—no truer evolutionist." Emerson advised: "Be an opener of doors to those who come after us." He was himself a tireless opener of doors for others. So were all the Transcendentalists.

Suggestions for Further Reading

Emerson and Thoreau are worth reading, rereading, and then reading again. Emerson, in particular, deserves and requires careful study. (I am one of the few people who today rate Emerson above Thoreau as thinker and artist.) He is not easy for the beginner. Carlyle complained that Emerson's sentences failed to "cohere"; they do not "rightly stick to their foregoers and their followers," he told Emerson; "the paragraphs are not as a beaten ingot, but as a beautiful bag of duck shot held together by canvas." Emerson admitted that the sentence was his unit and that his paragraphs were only collections of "infinitely repellent particles." Still, there is organic structure in all of Emerson's essays and a wonderful suggestiveness, and they yield fresh insights and new understanding with each rereading. Thoreau's style is more personal and concrete than Emerson's, and Thoreau was less interested than Emerson in philosophical abstractions. Yet in his own fashion he could handle large themes with ease and imagination, and one returns to him, as to Emerson, for both beauty and illumination. For the cluster of ideas making up American Transcendentalism Emerson and Thoreau are basic, and I have based this book largely on their writings.

There are many editions of the separate works of Emerson and Thoreau in both hard cover and paperback. The standard editions of Emerson's writings are: Edward W. Emerson, ed., *The Complete Works of Ralph Waldo Emerson* (12 vols., Boston, 1903-1904); E.W. Emerson and W.E. Forbes, eds., *The Journals of Ralph Waldo Emerson*

(10 vols., Boston and New York, 1909-1914); William H. Gilman *et al.*, eds., *The Journals and Miscellaneous Notebooks of Ralph Waldo Emerson* (Cambridge, 1960- —); Ralph L. Rusk, ed., *The Letters of Ralph Waldo Emerson* (6 vols., New York, 1939); C. E. Norton, ed., *The Correspondence of Thomas Carlyle and Ralph Waldo Emerson* (2 vols., Boston, 1883). For Thoreau, see *The Writings of Henry David Thoreau* (20 vols., Boston, 1906), and Walter Harding and Carl Bode, eds., *The Correspondence of Henry David Thoreau* (New York, 1958). The standard biography of Emerson is Ralph L. Rusk, *The Life of Ralph Waldo Emerson* (New York, 1949). It is also worth consulting James E. Cabot, *A Memoir of Ralph Waldo Emerson* (2 vols., Boston and New York, 1890); Edward W. Emerson, *Emerson in Concord, A Memoir* (Boston and New York, 1889); and perhaps the books on Emerson by Van Wyck Brooks, Moncure D. Conway, George W. Cooke, Oliver Wendell Holmes, Bliss Perry, Frank B. Sanborn, and Charles J. Woodberry. Milton Konvitz and Stephen Whicher have edited *Emerson, A Collection of Critical Essays* (Englewood Cliffs, N.J., 1962). The best biographical studies of Thoreau are Henry Seidel Canby, *Thoreau* (Boston, 1939), and Joseph Wood Krutch, *Henry David Thoreau* (New York, 1948). For critical essays on Thoreau, see Walter Harding, ed., *Thoreau: A Century of Criticism* (Dallas, 1954), and John H. Hicks, ed., *Thoreau in Our Season* (University of Massachusetts, 1962, 1966).

As for the other Transcendentalists, Perry Miller, ed., *The Transcendentalists: An Anthology* (Cambridge, 1950), is indispensable; it contains material taken from the writings of all the minor Transcendentalists, it covers just about every facet of the Transcendentalist movement, and its biographical notes and historical explanations are superb. Miller's is that *rara avis*, a creative anthology. Miller also edited a shorter collection, *The American Transcendentalists: Their Prose and Poetry* (Garden City, N.Y., 1957), which contains material not included in his longer volume. George Hochfield, ed., *Selected Writings of the American Transcendentalists* (Signet Classic, New York, 1961), is another useful paperbound collection, and it includes material not appearing in the Miller anthologies. With the two Miller books and Hochfield's collection the reader has a wide array of Transcendental material at his disposal; he should, however, supplement them with readings in Emerson and Thoreau, who are slighted in these anthologies to make room for the work of the less famous Transcendentalists. For the writings of individual Transcendentalists other than Emerson and Thoreau, see also Henry S. Commager, ed., *Theodore Parker, An Anthology* (Boston, 1960); Odell Shepard, ed., *The Journals of Bronson Alcott* (Boston, 1938); Perry Miller, ed., *Margaret Fuller, American Romantic* (Garden City, N.Y., 1963); Mason Wade, ed., *The Writings of Margaret Fuller* (New York, 1941); and Alvan S. Ryan, ed., *The Brownson Reader* (New York, 1955). The following biographies are standard: William I. Bartlett, *Jones Very, Emerson's "Brave Saint"* (Durham, N.C., 1942); Arthur S. Bolster, *James Freeman Clarke, Disciple to Advancing Truth* (Boston, 1954); Henry S. Commager, *Theodore Parker* (Boston, 1936); George W. Cooke, *John Sullivan Dwight* (Boston, 1898); Charles Crowe, *George Ripley, Transcendentalist and Utopian Socialist* (Athens, Ga., 1967); Joseph J. Deiss, *The Roman Years of Margaret Fuller* (New York, 1969); Edwin Gittleman, *Jones Very: The Effective Years* (New York, 1967); Orie W. Long, *Frederic Henry Hedge: A Cosmopolitan Scholar* (Portland, Maine, 1940); Theodore Maynard, *Orestes Brownson: Yankee, Radical, Catholic* (New York, 1943); Leonora Cranch Scott, *The Life and Letters of Christopher Pearse Cranch* (Boston, 1917); Arthur Schlesinger, Jr., *Orestes A. Brownson, A Pilgrim's Progress* (Boston, 1939); Odell Shepard, *Pedlar's Progress: The Life of Bronson Alcott* (Boston, 1937); Mason Wade, *Margaret Fuller: Whetstone of Genius* (New York, 1940); and John Weiss, *The Life and Correspondence of Theodore Parker* (2 vols., New York, 1864).

Among the best general studies of American Transcendentalism are the following: Octavius B. Frothingham, *Transcendentalism in New England: A History* (New York, 1876); Harold C. Goddard, *Studies in New England Transcendentalism* (New York, 1908); Clarence F. Gohdes, *The Periodicals of American Transcendentalism* (Durham, N.C., 1931); Alexander Kern, "The Rise of Transcendentalism," in Henry H. Clark, ed., *Transitions in American Literary History* (Durham, N.C., 1953); F. O. Matthiessen, *American Renaissance* (New York, 1941); Vernon L. Parrington, *Main Currents in American Thought* (3 vols., New York, 1927-1930), vol. II, *The Romantic Revolution in America*. There are two useful collections of critical essays on Transcendentalism: Myron Simon and Thornton H. Parsons, eds., *Transcendentalism and Its Legacy* (Ann Arbor, Mich., 1969), and George F. Whicher, ed., *The Transcendental Revolt* (rev. by Gail Kennedy, Lexington, Mass., 1968). For further suggestions for reading about American Transcendentalism, see Robert Spiller *et al.*, eds., *Literary History of the United States: Bibliography* (3rd ed.: revised, New York, 1963), 346-348.

Those wishing to explore further some of the themes treated in this book may want to examine (in addition to books mentioned in the text) some of the following special studies listed below. They represent only a tiny portion of the scholarly work already done on major Transcendental themes.

I. *Religious Radicalism*

Henry S. Commager, "Tempest in a Boston Tea Cup," *New England Quarterly*, VI (December, 1933), 651-675

David P. Edgell, "A Note on Channing's Transcendentalism," *New England Quarterly*, XXII (September, 1949), 394-397

Clarence H. Faust, "The Background of the Unitarian Opposition to Transcendentalism," *American Philology*, XXXV (1938), 297-324

Clarence Gohdes, "Some Remarks on Emerson's Divinity School Address," *American Literature*, I (1929-30), 27-31

Daniel Walker Howe, *The Unitarian Conscience, Harvard Moral Philosophy, 1805-1861* (Cambridge, 1970)

William R. Hutchison, *The Transcendental Ministers: Church Reform in the New England Renaissance* (Boston, 1959)

Arthur I. Ladu, "Channing and Transcendentalism," *American Literature*, XI (May, 1939), 29-37

Arthur R. Schultz and Henry A. Pochmann, "George Ripley: Unitarian, Transcendentalist, or Infidel?" *American Literature*, XIV (1942-43), 1-19

H. Shelton Smith, "Was Theodore Parker a Transcendentalist?" *New England Quarterly*, XXXVII (June, 1964), 147-170

D. Elton Trueblood, "The Influence of Emerson's Divinity School Address," *Harvard Theological Review*, XXXII (January, 1939), 41-56

Ronald V. Wells, *Three Christian Transcendentalists: James Marsh, Caleb Sprague Henry, Frederic Henry Hedge* (New York, 1943)

Conrad Wright, "Emerson, Barzillai Frost, and the Divinity School Address," *Harvard Theological Review*, XLIX (January, 1956), 19-43

*   *   *

II. *Intuitional Philosophy*

S. G. Brown, "Emerson's Platonism," *New England Quarterly*, XVIII (September, 1945), 325-345

Frederick I. Carpenter, *Emerson and Asia* (Cambridge, 1930)

Arthur E. Christy, *The Orient in American Transcendentalism* (New York, 1932)

Henry S. Commager, "The Dilemma of Theodore Parker," *New England Quarterly*, VI (June, 1933), 257-277

Merle Curti, "The Great Mr. Locke: America's Philosopher, 1783-1861," *Huntington Library Bulletin*, XI (1937), 107-155

Merrell R. Davis, "Emerson's 'Reason' and the Scottish Philosophers," *New England Quarterly*, XVII (June, 1944), 209-228

Lewis S. Feuer, "James Marsh and the Conservative Transcendentalist Philosophy, A Political Interpretation," *New England Quarterly*, XXXI (March, 1958), 3-31

John S. Harrison, *The Teachers of Emerson* (New York, 1910)

Harold S. Jantz, "German Thought and Literature in New England, 1620-1820," *Journal of English and Germanic Philology*, XLI (1942), 1-45

Alfred J. Kloeckner, "Intellect and Moral Sentiment in Emerson's Opinion of 'The Meaner Kinds' of Men," *American Literature*, XXX (1958-59), 322-338

Walter L. Leighton, *French Philosophers and New-England Transcendentalism* (Charlottesville, Virginia, 1908)

Frank MacShane, "Walden and Yoga," *New England Quarterly*, XXXVII (September, 1964), 322-342

George F. Newbrough, "Reason and Understanding in the Works of Theodore Parker," *South Atlantic Quarterly*, .XLVII (January, 1948), 64-75

Marjorie H. Nicolson, "James Marsh and the Vermont Transcendentalists," *The Philosophical Review*, XXXIV (January, 1925), 28-50

Henry A. Pochmann, *German Culture in America, Philosophical and Literary Influences* (Madison, Wisc., 1957)

Cameron Thompson, "John Locke and New England Transcendentalism," *New England Quarterly*, XXXV (December, 1962), 435-457

Frank T. Thompson, "Emerson and Carlyle," *Studies in Philology*, XXIV (July, 1927), 438-453

————, "Emerson's Indebtedness to Coleridge," *Studies in Philology*, XXIII (January, 1926), 55-76

Edgerly W. Todd, "Philosophical Ideas at Harvard College, 1817-1837," *New England Quarterly*, XVI (March, 1943), 63-90

William S. Vance, "Carlyle in America before *Sartor Resartus*," *American Literature*, VII (January, 1936), 363-375

Stanley M. Vogel, *German Literary Influences on the American Transcendentalists* (New Haven, 1955)

René Wellek, "Emerson and German Philosophy," *New England Quarterly*, XVI (1943), 41-62

————, "The Minor Transcendentalists and German Philosophy," *New England Quarterly*, XV (1942), 652-680

III. *Transcendental Idealism*

Joseph Warren Beach, "Emerson and Evolution," *University of Toronto Quarterly*, III (July, 1934), 474-497

Jonathan Bishop, *Emerson on the Soul* (Cambridge, 1964)

Frederick I. Carpenter, "William James and Emerson," *American Literature*, XI (1939-40), 39-57

Harry H. Clark, "Emerson and Science," *Philological Quarterly*, X (July, 1931), 225-255

Charles Mayo Ellis, *An Essay on Transcendentalism* (1842; ed. by Walter Harding, Gainesville, Fla., 1954)

Oscar W. Firkins, *Ralph Waldo Emerson* (Boston and New York, 1915)

Henry D. Gray, *A Statement of New England Transcendentalism as Expressed in the Philosophy of Its Chief Exponent* (Stanford, Calif., 1917)

Vivian C. Hopkins, *Spires of Form: A Study of Emerson's Aesthetic Theory* (Cambridge, 1951)

Edwin D. Mead, *The Influence of Emerson* (Boston, 1903)

Norman Miller, "Emerson's 'Each and All' Concept: A Reexamination," *New England Quarterly*, XLI (September, 1968), 381-392

Perry Miller, "From Edwards to Emerson," *New England Quarterly*, XIII (1940), 587-617

Sherman Paul, *Emerson's Angle of Vision* (Cambridge, 1952)

Joel Porte, "Nature as Symbol: Emerson's Noble Doubt," *New England Quarterly*, XXXVII (December, 1964), 453-476

Patrick F. Quinn, "Emerson and Mysticism," *American Literature*, XXI (1949-50), 397-414

Frank B. Sanborn, *The Genius and Character of Emerson* (Boston, 1884)

Carl F. Strauch, "Emerson's Sacred Science," *Publications of the Modern Language Society*, LXXIII (June, 1958), 237-250

George E. Woodberry, *Ralph Waldo Emerson* (New York, 1907)

IV. *Social Reform*

Robert C. Albrecht, "The Theological Response of the Transcendentalists to the Civil War," *New England Quarterly*, XXXVIII (March, 1965), 21-34

John T. Flanagan, "Emerson and Communism," *New England Quarterly*, X (June, 1937), 243-261

Nick Aaron Ford, "Henry David Thoreau, Abolitionist," *New England Quarterly*, XIX (September, 1946), 359-371

Margaret Fuller, *Woman in the Nineteenth Century* (ed. by Bernard Rosenthal, New York, 1971)

John C. Gerber, "Emerson and the Political Economists," *New England Quarterly*, XXII (September, 1949), 336-357

George Hendrick, "The Influence of Thoreau's 'Civil Disobedience' on Gandhi's *Satyagraha*," *New England Quarterly*, XXIX (December, 1956), 462-471

A. C. Kern, "Emerson and Economics," *New England Quarterly*, XIII (December, 1940), 678-696

Arthur I. Ladu, "Emerson: Whig or Democrat," *New England Quarterly*, XIII (September, 1940), 419-441

———, "The Political Ideas of Theodore Parker," *Studies in Philology*, XXXVIII (1941), 106-123

Dorothy McCuskey, *Bronson Alcott, Teacher* (New York, 1940)

Raymer McQuiston, *The Relation of Ralph Waldo Emerson to Public Affairs* (Lawrence, Kans., 1923)

Milton Meltzner, ed., *Thoreau: People, Principles, and Politics* (New York, 1963)

Perry Miller, "Emersonian Genius and the American Democracy," *New England Quarterly*, XXVI (March, 1953), 27-44

Marjory M. Moody, "The Evolution of Emerson as an Abolitionist," *American Literature*, XVII (1945-46), 1-21

Henry W. Sams, ed., *Autobiography of Brook Farm* (Englewood Cliffs, N.J., 1958)

Arthur W. Schlesinger, Jr., *The Age of Jackson* (Boston, 1945)

Clara E. Sears, *Bronson Alcott's Fruitlands* (Boston, 1915)

Rollo G. Silver, "Emerson as Abolitionist," *New England Quarterly*, VI (March, 1933), 154-158

Lindsay Swift, *Brook Farm* (New York, 1900)

V. *Cosmic Optimism*

William Braswell, "Melville as a Critic of Emerson," *American Literature*, IX (November, 1937), 317-334

Chester E. Jorgensen, "Emerson's Paradise Under the Shadow of Swords," *Philological Quarterly*, XI (July, 1932), 274-292

Roland F. Lee, "Emerson's 'Compensation' as Argument and as Art," *New England Quarterly*, XXXVII (September, 1964), 291-305

Maria Moravsky, "The Idol of Compensation," *Nation*, CXVIII (June 28, 1919), 1004-1005

Egbert S. Oliver, " 'Cock-a-Doodle-Doo!' and Transcendental Hocus-Pocus," *New England Quarterly*, XXI (June, 1948), 204-216

———, "Melville's Picture of Emerson and Thoreau in 'The Confidence Man,' " *College English*, VIII (November, 1946), 61-72

Henry F. Pommer, "The Contents and Basis of Emerson's Belief in Compensation," *Publications of the Modern Language Association*, LXXVII (June, 1962), 248-253

E. J. Rose, "Melville, Emerson, and the Sphinx," *New England Quarterly*, XXXVI (June, 1963), 249-258

Stephen E. Whicher, *Freedom and Fate, An Inner Life of Ralph Waldo Emerson* (Philadelphia, 1953)

Thomas R. Whitaker, "The Riddle of Emerson's 'Sphinx,' " *American Literature*, XXVII (1955-56), 179-195

VI. *Transience and Permanence*

Gay Wilson Allen, *The Solitary Singer, A Critical Biography of Walt Whitman* (New York, 1955)

William E. Bridges, "Transcendentalism and Psychotherapy," *American Literature*, XLI (1969-70), 157-177

John C. Broderick, "Thoreau's Proposals for Legislation," *American Quarterly*, VII (Fall, 1955), 285-290

Kenneth W. Cameron, ed., *Emerson Among His Contemporaries* (Hartford, Conn., 1967)

A. R. Caponigri, "Brownson and Emerson: Nature and History," *New England Quarterly*, XVIII (September, 1945), 368-390

John P. Diggins, "Thoreau, Marx, and the 'Riddle' of Alienation," *Social Research*, XXXIX (Winter, 1972), 571-598

G. R. Elliott, "On Emerson's 'Grace' and 'Self-Reliance,' " *New England Quarterly*, II (January, 1929), 93-104

Hubert H. Hoeltje, "Emerson, Citizen of Concord," *American Literature*, XI (1939-40), 367-378

Herman Hummel, "Emerson and Nietzsche," *New England Quarterly*, XIX (March, 1946), 63-84

John D. McCormick, "Emerson's Theory of Human Greatness," *New England Quarterly*, XXVI (September, 1953), 291-314

F. DeWolfe Miller, *Christopher Pearse Cranch and His Caricatures of New England Transcendentalism* (Cambridge, 1951)

John Brooks Moore, "Thoreau Rejects Emerson," *American Literature*, IV (1932-33), 241-256

Sherman Paul, *The Shores of America, Thoreau's Inward Exploration* (Urbana, Ill., 1958)

Joel Porte, *Emerson and Thoreau, Transcendentalists in Conflict* (Middleton, Conn., 1966)

————, "Emerson, Thoreau, and the Double Consciousness," *New England Quarterly*, XLI (March, 1968), 40-50

Rudolf Schottlaender, "Emerson and Nietzsche," *South Atlantic Quarterly*, XXXIX (July, 1940), 330-343

Leo Stoller, "Thoreau's Doctrine of Simplicity," *New England Quarterly*, XXIX (December, 1956), 443-461

Index